# ENDORSEM~~ENTS~~

Jeremiah Johnson is a Nathan to this Davidic generation and his standard for holiness and purity is a lifeline for this prophetic culture that's drowning in a sea of compromise and doctrinal error. Tears and groans are the earmark of this man's ministry and a holy awe follows him wherever he goes. The fear of the Lord grips me every time he speaks and I trembled with conviction as I read this book.

This book is a must read for every person genuinely called to the prophetic, and the *first* read to be taught in every prophetic school to ensure the pitfalls outlined in these pages aren't perpetuated in this current prophetic generation.

If your motives aren't pure and your life's mission isn't to become a martyr for being God's mouthpiece, then put this book down because it's not just a manuscript but an edict from the courtroom of heaven for all prophets or prophetic people. I believe this book will stand out as one reserved for the remnant of the seven thousand.

Alexander Pagani
Senior pastor of Amazing Church
Bestselling author of *The Secrets to Deliverance*

I've known, walked with, and ministered with Jeremiah Johnson many times over the last five years. His prophetic gifting is very evident and his words and dreams have shifted and anchored my own life in some of my most needed seasons. His gifting is evident, yet his gifting isn't what has left the greatest impact on me. It's been his passionate love of Jesus and prayer, his love for the Church, and his genuine love for people.

Rarely have I witnessed a prophetic person be able to marry grace and truth in such a striking way, and yet I've seen it in Jeremiah. I'm blown away with all that God has entrusted to him, and I believe it's because God is raising him up as a father in the body of Christ in this hour.

I cried as I read through this book, because of the tangible anointing on it. Jeremiah hits us with a lot of strong statements in this book, yet it's his broken spirit that I can feel on the other side of the pages. I pray that God uses this book in a mighty way to deliver the Church from the false and bring us forth into prophetic maturity.

Corey Russell·
Senior Leadership Team at IHOPKC
Author of *The Glory Within* and *Ancient Paths*

Jeremiah Johnson has a unique grasp on what God is doing in the prophetic work unfolding in this world-shaking period of history. He is one of the few who has clarified how different prophets have different spheres of authority and grace and calling. We all love the stories about Daniel, but few see that his prophetic ministry was to rulers in the sphere of government. He might not have been the most popular guest speaker at a conference and probably won't line people up for personal words.

As this book points out, the important thing is to know your sphere and shift things in the lane you are assigned to run in. Jeremiah's book is an extension of who he is. It's a tuning fork for those with a kindred spirit and a plumb line for those who are still seeking to make a name for themselves.

Jeremiah gives me hope that a powerful fresh breed of next generation prophetic is arising to make straight the way of the Lord. This book will align you for the great move of God that is coming upon us.

Dr. Lance Wallnau
Lance Learning Group

# CLEANSING & IGNITING THE
# PROPHETIC

## OTHER BOOKS BY JEREMIAH JOHNSON

*I See a New Prophetic Generation*

*I See a New Apostolic Generation*

*The Micaiah Company*

# CLEANSING & IGNITING THE

# PROPHETIC

## AN URGENT WAKE-UP CALL

JEREMIAH JOHNSON

DESTINY IMAGE® PUBLISHERS, INC.
P.O. Box 310, Shippensburg, PA 17257-0310
*"Promoting Inspired Lives."*

This book and all other Destiny Image and Destiny Image Fiction books are available at Christian bookstores and distributors worldwide.

Cover design by Eileen Rockwell

For more information on foreign distributors, call 717-532-3040.

Reach us on the Internet: www.destinyimage.com.

ISBN 13 TP: 978-0-7684-4623-4

ISBN 13 eBook: 978-0-7684-4624-1

ISBN 13 HC: 978-0-7684-4626-5

ISBN 13 LP: 978-0-7684-4625-8

For Worldwide Distribution, Printed in the U.S.A.

1 2 3 4 5 6 7 8 / 22 21 20 19 18

# DEDICATION

**T**O Leonard Ravenhill, A.W. Tozer, and David Wilkerson. Thank you for your unwavering stand for truth, righteousness, and the fear of the Lord. Your voices have greatly impacted my life, and I pray they will be reflected throughout this book and the prophetic generations to come. Without holiness, the Church has nothing to say to the world.

# CONTENTS

FOREWORD BY MICHAEL L. BROWN .............................13

INTRODUCTION BY RICK JOYNER................................17

CHAPTER 1   THE ROAD TO EMMAUS.........................................23

CHAPTER 2   THE EMERGING PROPHETS OF FIRE.............................29

CHAPTER 3   THE SONS AND DAUGHTERS SHALL PROPHESY .....................35

CHAPTER 4   DELUSIONS OF PROPHETIC GRANDEUR............................41

CHAPTER 5   THE GIFT OF PROPHECY.......................................49

CHAPTER 6   THE PROPHET'S PROFILE......................................57

CHAPTER 7   MY PROPHETIC JOURNEY.......................................65

CHAPTER 8   THE HYPER-GRACE PROPHETIC MOVEMENT ......................79

CHAPTER 9   UNAUTHORIZED PROPHETIC MINISTRY...........................93

CHAPTER 10  DANGER IN SUPERNATURAL PROPHETIC EVANGELISM ...............99

CHAPTER 11  PROPHETIC MINISTRY IN THE LOCAL CHURCH....................105

CHAPTER 12  THE PITFALLS OF THE PROPHET'S MINISTRY ...................115

CHAPTER 13  PROPHETS AND THE FIVE-FOLD MINISTRY ......................129

CHAPTER 14    A VISION OF THE COMING DAYS ................................ 135

              AFTERWORD BY R. LOREN SANDFORD .......................... 149

              NOTES ................................................ 153

# FOREWORD

**I**N 1988, after attending a leadership meeting where visiting prophets ministered to those in attendance, I returned home sensing something was wrong. Something was missing. Many of the words were quite accurate, that was true. But every single word was overwhelmingly positive, and virtually every leader was going to have a megachurch in the future. A few were also going to raise the dead!

And under no circumstances did any of the visiting prophets feel the need to step away from the mic, take one of the pastors aside, and minister to him in private. Instead, men whom we knew were struggling seriously and hardly fit to be in the ministry received wonderful, glorious words.

Not long after that meeting, I felt the Lord speak a powerful word to me about prophetic ministry. In light of this very important book written by Jeremiah, it seems right to share it here:

> "I want prophets," says the Lord, "who will know My heart and not just My voice, My ways and not just My words, My pain and not just My power. I *want*," says the Lord, "prophets."

> "But where are the Elijahs of *God*?" says the God of Elijah; "where are *My* men? Where are the *interces-*

*sors* who *hear* and speak?" says the Lord, "the prophets who moan and weep? Everybody is running," says the Lord, "everybody is running—but I have not sent them all. Everybody has a message," says the Lord, "everybody has their pet. But *I* have a burden," says the Lord, "and *I* have a word. And *My* word pulls down powers of darkness, and *My* word consumes; *My* word is full of My life, and *My* word heals. MY Word," says the Lord.

"For there are prophets and there are prophets," says the Lord, "and I called men prophets in My Word who were not even prophets at all. [For those who bring oracles in My name are called prophets.] Now if these men who were not even prophets were called prophets, don't let it disturb you if I call men prophets today who are only partially prophets."

Now, 30 years later, Jeremiah Johnson has written a sharp, clear, brokenhearted, God-loving exposition of these very same words. How my own heart resonates with his writing! And Jeremiah has done it with accuracy, addressing many problems within the contemporary prophetic movement while pointing to Word-based solutions. And in all that he writes, he is jealous for the well-being of the local church.

Throughout this book, Jeremiah is constantly calling us back to the Word, constantly turning our attention to Jesus, constantly urging us to submit to God's standards, constantly showing that the Word and the Spirit and the character of Christ must always be in harmony and that humility and the fear of the Lord are even more important than the anointing. And throughout this book, he reminds that the message of repentance is foundational for all true prophetic ministry. How did we ever forget this?

Like Jeremiah, I too believe that God is preparing to do something amazing and far greater than anything we have witnessed so far. But that means that we must set our own houses in order. And since prophetic ministry is very powerful, not to mention very precious in the Lord's eyes, it is essential that we address abuses and problems in our movement.

As you read the pages that follow, I believe your own heart will burn with holy jealousy, as does Jeremiah's, and I believe you will lose any taste for hyper-grace prophets or manipulative prophets or mercenary prophets or prideful prophets. Instead, you'll look for those who come out of the secret place with a message from the throne of God. Oh, that the Lord might raise up such a mighty company in our day!

May the word on fire burn afresh in your own heart and life as you read this vitally important book. And, although Jeremiah is still a young man, I couldn't think of a better person to write these words. He lives what he preaches and preaches what he lives. And he ends with a vision of great hope for the future. I affirm that vision with him.

Michael L. Brown, Ph.D.
Host of the Line of Fire radio broadcast
Author of *Playing with Holy Fire:*
*A Wakeup Call to the Pentecostal-Charismatic Church*

# INTRODUCTION BY RICK JOYNER

THERE are few things that can ignite passion and zeal for the Lord and His work like authentic prophetic ministry. In the Book of Ezra we see that the work of restoring the house of God ceased until Haggai and Zechariah the prophets started prophesying. It says in Ezra 6:14 that "the elders of the Jews were successful in building through the prophesying of Haggai the prophet and Zechariah the son of Iddo." This is a prophetic parallel of where the Church is today. Many had the vision of seeing the Church restored to all of its glory but got discouraged and distracted from the work. It will require the prophets to arise as Haggai and Zechariah did to again awaken and inspire the people to finish the work they began.

Just as there are few things that can inspire zeal for the Lord and His purposes as authentic prophetic ministry, there are few things that can be more devastating to the work of the Lord than false or pseudo prophetic ministry. Therefore a key issue is how do we recognize and receive from the real, and how do we recognize and reject the false.

We see in Scripture that virtually every prophet of God had to deal with false prophets. We can also note that there were many more false prophets than true ones. We also can see that in virtually every case the false ones were prophesying what the people, or the leaders, wanted to hear, and the true prophets often stood alone with their counterpoint.

So how do we distinguish the real from the false? How do we receive the true and reject the false? This should begin with recognizing that this will not be easy because Satan is a skilled counterfeiter. Even more challenging is how the Lord seemed to want to make distinguishing the true from the false difficult. When the devil sowed tares in the midst of His wheat, His command was to "let them grow up together." Why would God do this?"

In the Parable of the Wheat and Tares we have several important factors. First, the Lord only planted the wheat; the tares were planted by the devil. There are some whom the Lord sends, and there are some whom the devil sends. Even so, we must consider that the only way the devil could have done this is for the Lord to allow it. Why would He allow it? It seems that learning to deal with tares is part of His curriculum for His people. This is likely a reason why He would even allow someone like Judas in His own inner circle.

Second, the Lord said to let the wheat and the tares grow up together so that the wheat will not be damaged when we try to separate them. Many prophets whom the Lord sent carry the wounds caused by the disregard of the Lord's command to let the wheat and tares grow together by leaders who thought they were wise enough to discern between the wheat and tares before they matured. Many of these leaders would end up throwing out the wheat, and keeping the tares, and then blame the prophetic movement for the chaos they caused by their own works.

Wheat and tares look so much alike that it is almost impossible to distinguish them before they mature. Those who are true can be just as arrogant, foolish, and sinful as the tares until they mature. The main way that wheat and tares are distinguished at "the harvest," or when both have matured, is that the wheat will bow over and the tares remain standing upright. This is a metaphor for how the true grow in humility and the false grow in pride. If one is maturing but getting more resistant to correction, we have a problem. God resists the proud, but gives His grace to the humble (see James 4:6; 1 Pet. 5:5). We are told throughout Proverbs that the wise love correction and reproof, but the foolish hate it. So, watching those who are more prone to embrace and appreciate correction and those who are not can tell us a lot.

These are general principles, but there are additional factors, such as if the correction is valid or from a valid authority. It is right to resist correction from invalid authority. Many Christians live in perpetual defeat because they wrongly accept the devil's condemnation as correction from God.

Others get misled because they receive guidance or correction from other Christians who may have the best intentions but are illegitimate because they have presumed authority that was not given to them from the Lord—the only Source of true authority in the kingdom. A good example of this is the media, even "Christian" media. Being a journalist does not give one authority in the Church. Neither does being a good writer or speaker. God established leaders such as apostles, elders, pastors, etc. as authorities in His Church. Most of those who fall into this presumption and become illegitimate judges of the Church become "fault-finders," and as we see in Jude a special judgement is reserved for them we should all fear.

Even those authorities appointed by God have specific "spheres" of authority that are based on experience and fruitfulness. The apostle Paul explained to the Corinthians that if he was not an apostle to others, he was to them because they were his fruit, an obvious result of his authority. So Paul was admitting that he was not an authority to everyone, and he wasn't. For example, he was not an apostle to the Jews, as the Lord had given that sphere to Peter. As Paul also related to the Corinthians, he had authority for building them up or tearing them down, by which we can conclude that we do not have authority to tear down what we have not been used to build.

Therefore we should ask those who presume to be judges and critics, journalists or presumed prophets, what they have built that gives them the authority to tear down. As a publisher we all too frequently receive manuscripts by authors who claim to have the new wineskin pattern for the Church. My first question to them is to show me the ones that they have been used to raise up. To date, none have been able to show me such a work, and therefore we have not published any such books. Authority comes from having fruit, not theories.

There are many books available on releasing the prophetic or raising up prophets. Some are legitimate because you can go to their work and find fruitful and maturing prophetic ministries. Others you go to have none, so why should we listen to them?

There are also books written seeking to bring correction to prophetic ministry by those who are not prophets, and admit to not being overseers of prophets. One well-known teacher recounted in a book many horror stories of the way supposed prophetic people wounded others or damaged churches. I have been around prophetic people for nearly 50 years now, and I have not heard anything as extreme as some of these stories, so I called the author to check some of these out. He asserted that every story was related to him by a pastor. I then asked if he went to the so-called prophetic people in any of these cases to hear their side of it, as there is almost always another side to every account. He had not done this. When I asked for the sources so I could check them out he would not provide them. As I continued to press this I became convinced that these stories were either made up or greatly embellished, and the book did great damage to the Church as we would expect.

The Pharisees had a legitimate question when they asked Jesus by what authority He did His works. Jesus commended the Ephesian church in Revelation 3 for having put to the test those who call themselves apostles and were not. We can expect that He would give the same commendation for those who put to the test any authority to distinguish the legitimate from the illegitimate. Whenever we tolerate the illegitimate we are allowing a terrible devaluation of our spiritual currency, not to mention allowing a wide-open gate of hell through which the Church will certainly be assaulted.

Even if someone has built a large work, if they want to bring correction on the prophetic I would first like to see what they have done to raise up prophets. There is a saying that "Any jackass can kick a barn down, but it takes a skillful carpenter to build one." The apostle corrected the Corinthians for honoring authorities who "slapped them in the face," and abused them but for not recognizing Paul's authority even though he was the one who had been used to build them into the church that they were. Immature or carnal people will respond to carnal or even abusive authority faster than they tend to recognize true builders.

We must not continue to pay attention to people unless they have fruit of their own to verify their wisdom. That is basically what Jesus said when He told us that we would know them by their fruit. It is not just what people say but what they have done that establishes true spiritual authority.

So what gives Jeremiah Johnson the authority to say the things he has written in this book? First, maturity is not just the result of age or time served. I have met many Christians who have been so for decades and are still spiritually immature. Maturity requires experience, but experience alone does not result in maturity. Maturing comes from having the wisdom to learn from experience. Just as there are some who may have been Christians for a long time but remain immature, some mature far beyond their years by their wisdom and how they handle experience.

Jeremiah Johnson is one who I think has a maturity far beyond his age. I think much of this can be attributed to how he got engaged at a young age in building a church and helping to raise up other prophetic ministries. There is a wisdom and a maturity that comes from building something that reading a multitude of books cannot duplicate.

I was a pilot by profession. I liken the way some are given influence in the body of Christ to accepting someone as the pilot of a commercial jet even though they have never actually flown a plane, but they have read a lot of books on the subject. Would you get on such a flight? No, because your life would certainly be in jeopardy if you did. Should we not be just as concerned for our spiritual life? We must heed the biblical exhortation to "know those who labor among us."

What Jeremiah Johnson has written in this book can be helpful in evaluating those who claim to be prophets and their messages. This is not all-inclusive but provides a good foundation to start with. It comes from one who is actually engaged in the work, has been for some time, and already has fruit that can be measured. He is one prophets can look to and say "He's one of us." He's also one pastors and church leaders can look at and say, "He's one of us."

Even a skillful carpenter sometimes must tear down a faulty foundation before a good one can be built. There are mindsets and even teachings in some prophetic circles that need to be torn down, and Jeremiah does not shy away from them in this book. There are others that are off, but just need adjusting. I'm impressed by how he already seems to have the wisdom to know the difference and address them accordingly. That is the sign of one whom I believe will emerge as one of the true "master-builders" in these times.

# CHAPTER 1

# THE ROAD TO
# EMMAUS

**G**OD is raising up end-time prophetic messengers who will proclaim Jesus Christ and all of His glory to the ends of the earth. Even now, these lovesick forerunners are preparing the Bride to meet their Bridegroom King. The Word of God burns inside of them like fire in their bones that they cannot contain. They are daily experiencing intimate encounters with the Son of God as they sit with Him and learn how to meditate upon His Word day and night.

These sons and daughters will help usher in revival to the Church centered upon the knowledge of God and encountering the person of Jesus. This company of burning and shining lamps will devour the Word of God. They will say "yes" to fresh encounters on the road to Emmaus where the unveiling of Christ will be made known to them through the Law, the Psalms, the Prophets, and the New Testament. As these prophetic messengers learn to walk the road to Emmaus, they will continually invite others to join them on this incredible pursuit of the truth that can only be found in God's Word.

Is your heart burning within you to personally encounter the glorious person of Jesus Christ and make Him known to the world around you? Revelation 19:10 says, "the testimony of Jesus is the spirit of prophecy." In other words, when the spirit of prophecy begins to move among a fellowship of believers, they will begin to declare with a passionate and burning heart cry who Jesus Christ really is to a generation.

In Luke 24, two disciples were walking to a village called Emmaus as they discussed the events that surrounded the life, ministry, death, and even resurrection of Jesus. As they were conversing, suddenly Jesus Himself approached and began traveling with them. Luke 24:16 records, "But their eyes were prevented from recognizing Him."

Jesus was walking right beside these two disciples, yet they could not see Him for who He really was. They began to tell Him about His own life and ministry, not even realizing who they were talking to. After some time, Jesus began to explain Himself to them through the Scriptures and eventually even reclined at a table and broke bread and gave it to them.

Instantly, Jesus vanished before them and their eyes were finally open! They said, "Were not our hearts burning within us while He was speaking to us on the road, while He was explaining the Scriptures to us?" (Luke 24:32).

We have to ask ourselves, what is the primary way that Jesus Christ Himself chose to reveal who He was to these disciples after He rose again? He clearly decided to do it through His written Word. He walked and talked with two disciples who knew about Him but who didn't really know Him.

# A REVIVAL OF THE WORD OF GOD

Some of our churches today have become full of people who are spiritually starving while stuffed with every physical comfort and pleasure. We have in many ways successfully birthed a churchgoing generation that is addicted to video games, movies, and entertainment but has no real appetite for the word of God. Jeremiah cried out to his generation and said, "Behold, the word of the Lord is a reproach to you; you have no delight in it" (see Jer. 6:10).

In the midst of this crisis where the Bible has become a reproach to many Christians and they no longer take delight in it, God is raising up a generation of plumb-line prophets who are going to help the body of Christ rediscover hearing, delighting in, trembling before, and obeying the Word of God. A bored generation of churchgoers who are desperately searching for ways to get through their quiet times with God are going to encounter prophetic messengers who burn with the fire of God's Word in their bellies.

I see a hungry and growing remnant of saints and church leaders who will absolutely love the Word of God and build their lives and ministries upon it. Plumb-line prophets are emerging who will be used mightily in a spirit of wisdom and revelation to enlighten the eyes of the Church to the power found in the Bible. There is a man who lives between the lines of Scripture; His name is Jesus. Many Christians say, "I know that verse" but my question is, "Does that verse know you?"

# OVEREMPHASIS ON PERSONAL PROPHECY

I'm deeply concerned that in some parts of the contemporary prophetic movement there is an overemphasis on giving out personal prophecy at the expense of preaching and teaching the Word of God. I have had multiple pastors and saints at different conferences and churches throughout the world tell me, "Put down your Bible and prophesy to us."

If we drift from the foundation of the Word of God in the contemporary prophetic movement, we will create a generation of prophetic people who are hungry to be stimulated with words of blessing but who do not want to get impregnated with the truth of God's Word. Many will hunger for personal prophecy but reject the foundation and place of encounter in the Bible. We must have prophets and prophetic people who want more than to be tickled with promises of destiny and wealth. We must be provoked into holy and righteous living through biblical teaching and preaching.

I see God raising up plumb-line prophets in the earth who are going to teach and encourage a generation to primarily give themselves to the study of the revealed will of God found in Scripture and less time chasing after the hidden will of God oftentimes revealed in experiences. We desperately need to see the Word of God handled accurately and with integrity in the contemporary prophetic movement.

## THE PLUMB LINE

While the two disciples were on the road to Emmaus, Jesus chose to use the Law, the Psalms, and the Prophets to reveal Himself to them. There were not portions of Scripture that Jesus threw away simply because they could be potentially offensive. As the body of Christ experiences a revival of the Word of God, there will be a company of plumb-line prophets emerging who are going to preach and prophesy Genesis through Revelation.

One of the greatest mistakes we can make in the contemporary prophetic movement is to limit our revelation of who God is based on our personal experiences alone and not according to the full counsel of God as revealed in the Bible. For example, some prophetic people have had deep personal encounters with the goodness and kindness of God, but from their experience, and therefore erroneously, they portray God as if He is only good and kind. They categorically reject any idea of the correction, discipline, and rebuke of the Lord because that has not been their personal experience.

The plumb-line prophets are going to bring greatly needed balance to the contemporary prophetic movement as they will preach and prophesy directly from the Word of God. There will be no aspects of God's character and nature that they will hide from burning hearts who are desperate to encounter Jesus Christ.

Several years ago, I ministered at a church that was well known for hosting prophets from all over the world. They advertised the meetings online, and at every session there was not a single seat open in the entire building. As we began to worship, God spoke to me immediately and said, "Jeremiah, My people have come for personal prophecy as they have for many years in this place, but they do not want to hear My written Word taught and preached. I now forbid you from giving any personal prophecies this weekend." Immediately my heart stopped as I knew how disappointed the people would be who had driven and flown in from all over the country to be at these prophetic gatherings.

For six sessions on that weekend, I preached and taught out of the Word of God with everything I had and prophesied to no one. The altars were packed every night as God was calling His people to repentance and prayer. After the conference, the pastor came up to me with an incredible smile on his face. He said, "Son, we have been hosting prophetic conferences here for more than 25 years. This is the first time ever where the Word of God was preached and no personal prophecy was given. Without hesitation, I can tell you that this was the best prophetic conference we have ever had." I was stunned. He then handed me a love offering and said, "This is the largest love offering we have ever received for a guest speaker. The people were truly transformed and moved by the power that is truly found in the Word of God. Thanks for coming."

On the plane ride home from that weekend I cried my eyes out. The people not only gave extremely generously, but I knew God blessed my obedience to follow His voice in that moment. Could a revival of the Word of God truly be coming to the contemporary prophetic movement?

Many of the prophetic words that God wants to release over His people in this hour have nothing to do with what we are going to receive and everything to do with who we are becoming. We are going to witness a rise of prophetic words that are directly geared toward assisting people in partnering with their ultimate call in life: "to be transformed into the image and likeness of the Son" (see Rom. 8:29).

Unless we wholeheartedly give ourselves as prophets and prophetic people to embracing every aspect of God's character and nature as revealed in Scripture, we will not only limit Him but also misrepresent Him to people.

There is a road to Emmaus being unveiled to this generation. God is calling His people to fresh encounters in the Word of God. Plumbline prophets are rising who will preach and prophesy out of the Law, the Psalms, the Prophets, and the New Testament. These prophetic messengers will burn with fresh fire and zeal to anchor the Church in the knowledge of God. An igniting of the contemporary prophetic movement is coming, and the source of that fire is going to be the restoration of the full counsel of God's Word.

# CHAPTER 2

# THE EMERGING PROPHETS OF
# FIRE

I see prophets of fire emerging in the contemporary prophetic movement who have had their motives and intentions cleansed and ignited like never before. God has been preparing them in the wilderness and training them in brokenness and humility. Self-promotion and delusions of prophetic grandeur have been purged out of these messengers through trial and testing. The emerging prophets of fire understand their assignment and will not move outside the jurisdiction God has given them. They will not allow themselves to be treated like vending machines but will speak only when God speaks.

The emerging prophets of fire will not be lone rangers. They will not carry bitterness, anger, and unforgiveness toward the body of Christ. In fact, they will operate from such a place of purity and humility that they will be accepted in numerous churches and ministries around the world. The prophetic words they release will be difficult for some to receive, but as these messages are given in the right spirit and with the right heart God will multiply their impact.

# THE OBADIAHS OF CHURCH LEADERSHIP

The emerging prophets of fire will be specifically received and accepted in numerous churches and ministries by what I call the "Obadiahs." These will be pastors and leaders who will provide safety and a special grace to host and accommodate the prophets of fire because they understand the call on their lives. It was Obadiah who hid the prophets in a cave during the reign of Ahab and Jezebel.

The Obadiahs of church leadership will understand the difference between believers who operate in the gift of prophecy and those who are called to be prophets of God. They will welcome the prophets of fire to come and expose, uproot, and tear down carnality and faulty foundations that are contrary to the character and Word of God. The Obadiahs and the emerging prophets of fire will have a very unique and special relationship as they will bring healing and deliverance to one another.

# PROPHETIC WARNING

If the prophets of fire are not careful to remain purified and walk with humility, they will have the tendency to operate outside the body of Christ because of bitterness and past hurt. This is not God's will for their lives. Dangerous prophets and prophetic people are those who reject any form of accountability and community. The prophets of fire will be directly connected to a body of believers and walk in close relationships with church leadership because they are friends of the Bridegroom.

## COUNTERBALANCE IS NEEDED

The prophets of fire are going to restore necessary counterbalance to the body of Christ and the contemporary prophetic movement as they function and operate in the grace God has given them. We will no longer just have building and planting, encouragement and blessing, but there will be correction, rebuke, uprooting, tearing down, overthrowing, and destroying when necessary. It will be a glorious display of true prophetic ministry that reflects the ministry of Jesus Christ (see Rev. 19:10). We are going to see prophets of fire weep as they call the body of Christ to repentance. We are going to see fiery messengers who have been sent to confront and remove the spot and wrinkle from the Bride prior to the return of the Bridegroom.

Perhaps Wendy Alec saw these prophets of fire emerging when she wrote and said:

> God says, I am raising up a company of prophets who will act as an abrasion to the body of Christ, for surely there are many of My servants who will even question and wonder at the manner in which My prophets have been called to walk in these days. Their faces are set like flint and they will not heed the voice or the system of politics and the manipulations of men. They shall one by one come forth in this time.
>
> And they shall not need or require man's favor or reward, for they are a strange and wonderful breed dedicated and holy unto the Lord. They are neither bribable nor corruptible. Their master is neither mammon nor fame, but the Holy One of Israel. These

prophets will come forth with a fierce countenance, for they do not listen to the voice of man. They have been trained in the desert place and the wilderness and have been raised on misunderstanding and rejections. They will not be bought by men or ministries. They shall raise their voices against the false systems of My Church. And they shall raise their hand even as Elijah, and My signs and My judgments shall come forth.

Many church leaders will stand back in wonder and receive this terrible company of prophets, for fear and conviction will overtake them. Take care and discern correctly that you may not be found having despised these strange and terrible ones, the prophets of the Most High.

## CLEANSING JUDGMENT

God is coming to cleanse and ignite the contemporary prophetic movement. The prophets of fire are being released. The place of intercession and prayer is going to be the safeguard and protection for these messengers. Jeremiah said, "If they be prophets...let them now make intercession to the Lord of hosts" (Jer. 27:18 KJV). One of the primary earmarks of the prophets of fire will be the amount of time they spend in the secret place. They will actually crave and prefer the prayer room over any stage and microphone.

The body of Christ needs its prophetic voices to be holy, pure, and functioning at full strength in order to play the role God wants them to play in this strategic time in the history of the world. Look for cleansing fire to sweep the contemporary prophetic movement in the days ahead. Prophets of fire are emerging who will carry a purified heart and desire to see prayer, intimacy, and unity restored to the Church.

# CHAPTER 3

# THE SONS AND DAUGHTERS SHALL
# PROPHESY

**T**HERE has never been a greater need in history than now for healthy and mature prophets and prophetic people to emerge in the earth. A very clear and distinct sound must come forth so that the body of Christ can prepare herself for these last days prior to the return of Jesus Christ. There has been an army of prophets and prophetic people that God has been training in hiddenness and purifying their motives and ministries for such a time as this.

There is a unique urgency and tears that come with the passion and burden to see prophetic ministry cleansed and ignited. It is a special groan being released by God Himself for authentic, accountable, and purified prophetic ministry to truly manifest in the body of Christ. We must have the accurate word and heart of God delivered to this generation by messengers who have character that matches the prophetic anointing upon their lives.

I recently received a heart-wrenching phone call from a well-known leader in the body of Christ. As I picked up the phone, I heard the unique groan and urgency in his voice that I described above. "Jeremiah," he said, and then suddenly paused. "Where are the real prophets?"

I said, "What do you mean? I know you as one who is constantly surrounded by prophets and prophetic people."

"No, that's not what I'm talking about," he said. "I'm asking where are the prophets and prophetic people who are going to deliver us the real words and heart of God? Not the kind that gets you more fame, fortune, and influence. Jeremiah," he said as he choked back tears, "we desperately need prophetic words that are actually going to challenge, correct, and rebuke the body of Christ if necessary. I'm not hearing any of them at all anymore. What has happened to the contemporary prophetic movement? Who is responsible for all this flattery, all this pampering, and all this stroking?"

## THE GOODNESS AND SEVERITY OF GOD

Long ago, Isaiah prophesied that days would come when glory and crisis, light and darkness would cover the whole earth (see Isa. 60). I was asked last year on national television which one it is. The exact question was, "Jeremiah, are we living in days of great darkness or light? Is it glory or crisis?"

I responded, "Both!" and silence fell upon the audience. Could God's Word actually be true?

I believe God has specifically revealed to me that the clarion call that will come forth from prophets and prophetic people in the days ahead will be very unique in that it will highlight every aspect of who God is. I was given a powerful prophetic dream several months ago that illustrates this word well.

In the dream, I was invited to a meeting between Bill Johnson from Redding, California, and David Wilkerson who passed some years ago. Bill was wearing a t-shirt that said, "The goodness of God" and David was wearing a shirt that said, "The severity of God." Both men were very fond of each other and were exchanging powerful stories based upon the revelation they had been given. God spoke to me in the dream and said, "Jeremiah, I am going to marry My goodness and My severity in one generation, for the dirge and the dance will be played simultaneously all over the earth."

I woke up from the prophetic dream with the heavy presence of God in my bedroom. As I lay in my bed, the word *polarizing* came to my mind and heart. I said, "God, only a mature people will be able to receive messengers of Your goodness and kindness as well as Your severity and holiness."

He said, "Yes! In one place I will release the fear of who I am and in another place I will release My oil of joy. In one place I will release the fire of My holiness, and in another place they will weep as I release My mercy and grace."

I foresee many places in the body of Christ being prepared even now for a tremendous last-days outpouring. The sons and daughters are going to prophesy, dream dreams, and have incredible visions. In other places in the body of Christ, I foresee them being shaken and turned upside down by the holiness and fear of the Lord. Great repentance, exposing of sin, and encounters with the holiness and discipline of God await them. Can the body of Christ mature to the place where we are willing to receive all these different manifestations and displays of the character and nature of God? I believe we must if we are going to step into all God has promised in His Word in these last days.

When I refer to "igniting" the prophetic, I am specifically referring to the promise of Joel 2 being released in the earth. We are going to witness an unprecedented wave of dreams, visions, and prophecy mark the end-time Church. An explosion of the prophetic spirit is going to mantle large parts of the body of Christ. The sheep are going to be instructed in hearing the voice of the Shepherd, and great blessing will come because of it.

When I refer to "cleansing" the prophetic, I am intentionally referring to the damage, abuse, and immaturity that for the large part has gone unchecked for years within the prophetic movement. This book seeks to address both the need for the cleansing and igniting of the prophetic and the urgency that comes with it. We are going to see a fresh release of God's Spirit in some churches and ministries, and in others there is going to be restraint as purging and cleansing is necessary. In some churches and ministries the saints are going to freely prophesy and encourage one another, but in other places it is time to judge and hold those accountable who have been giving inaccurate prophetic words for years. In some churches and ministries the prophetic must be constantly invited and welcomed, but in other churches and ministries the prophetic needs to be married to a lifestyle of consecration and separation from the things of the world. In some churches and ministries great leaps of faith in the prophetic are coming, but in other churches and ministries the prophetic has become a mere game and needs to purified.

If ever there was a time in history for igniting and cleansing the prophetic, it is now! We must see the prophetic spirit ignited in believers, churches, and ministries everywhere. We desperately need people who are seeing and hearing what the Spirit of God is saying and doing. Every sphere of society must be infiltrated with everyday believers who listen and obey the voice of God at all costs. We need prophetic ministry that is cleansed, accurate, and done with the right motives and intentions. Authentic prophetic ministry released with true accountability and purity will be a hammer in the hands of the Lord that will break up the fallow ground of the world around us and release the fire of God that cannot be quenched or satisfied. It's time for the sons and daughters to prophesy.

# CHAPTER 4

# DELUSIONS OF PROPHETIC
# GRANDEUR

I is with much prayer, brokenness, and tears that I would like to suggest that parts of the contemporary prophetic movement have become sick and are in need of serious purging and deep cleansing. We live in an unprecedented time in history when more individuals are claiming to be "prophets" and having the "word of the Lord" than ever before. Even more frightening is how easy it has now become to gain platforms and popularity in parts of the body of Christ without a proven history of character, accuracy, or perhaps even a legitimate prophetic anointing. At worst, I'm deeply troubled that we are witnessing the rise and acceptance of false prophets leading the body of Christ astray and at best we are now calling people "prophets" who really just have the gift of prophecy that brings general encouragement and blessing.

As I continue to travel and minister prophetically around the United States and the world every year, I see firsthand how these latest trends and mistakes are causing confusion, doubt, and more questions than answers for many involved in prophetic ministry. I'm convinced that we desperately need not only real prophets of God to take their stand in the body of Christ, but we are in dire need of an igniting and cleansing of contemporary prophetic ministry.

In my agony, brokenness, and fervent cries to God, I seem to be able to find comfort only in the fact that the contemporary prophetic movement of our day directly mirrors the days of old that Jeremiah lived in. How relieving it is to me to know that nothing "new" under the sun is happening in the earth right now concerning prophetic ministry. In Jeremiah's day, he said that the prophets were prophesying when God had not spoken to them and they were traveling and ministering when God had not even sent them (see Jer. 23:21). I believe the words of Jeremiah the prophet ring terribly true for the days that we now live in.

## THE PROPHET'S FREE-FOR-ALL

The explosion of social media outlets has given many prophets and prophetic people a platform that God has never given them. On more than five occasions, I have interacted with individuals who marketed themselves as "national prophets," but upon meeting with them they did not even have grace to function prophetically on a local level. Unfortunately, having meetings where ten to twenty people attend weekly does not make someone a "national prophet." I don't care how good they make their flyers look or what title they put in front of their name on their business card.

We have prophets and prophetic people who are stealing other leaders' words and publishing them on social media to make it look like they carry revelation when really it's someone else's (see Jer. 23:30). Where is the integrity in the contemporary prophetic movement to cite the real source of the so-called "revelations" and "prophecies" that we are sharing with the masses? In one bizarre case, a popular prophet in America was caught reading a psychic's horoscope word for word publicly and acting like it was the prophetic word God gave him for that year. How terrifying!

From my perspective, traveling prophetic ministry has largely become the latest pipe dream of too many prophets and prophetic people in the contemporary prophetic movement who are filled with delusions of prophetic grandeur.

For example, I encountered a "prophet" last year who was so desperate to have a traveling prophetic ministry that he would call pastors around the clock trying to get a meeting and would even offer to cover his own expenses. After one year of this "prophet" developing a full travel itinerary by constantly contacting pastors, he found himself in debt more than 38 thousand dollars. To the outside world, it looked like this person had a flourishing traveling prophetic ministry. The truth, however, was that through self-promotion and selfish ambition, this individual got himself into serious debt all because he had an "itch" God never gave him. I wish I could say this was an isolated incident, but I have encountered these types of self-promoting ministers again and again.

How can we start the cleansing and purification process that the contemporary prophetic culture so desperately needs? How can we see genuine prophetic ministry ignited in our midst? We know we can't throw out prophetic ministry altogether as some are in the habit of doing, out of their disillusionment and disappointment, but we must come to terms with the fact that God is coming in this hour to cleanse and ignite His prophets and this most precious ministry that He has given the body of Christ. Furthermore, before Jesus comes for His Bride, He is coming to His Bride, and those days are quickly upon us. The contemporary prophetic movement must be purified, cleansed, and washed of all impurity and wickedness before Jesus Christ returns.

I believe that one of the primary ways that we can begin the cleanup so urgently needed in the contemporary prophetic movement is by strongly encouraging and challenging true prophets of God and prophetic people to learn how to stay in their lane and jurisdiction. We must see prophets and prophetic people commissioned and sent forth in their specific sphere of authority and influence.

# PROPHETS: STAY IN YOUR LANE

Throughout my travels ministering prophetically across the USA and many nations of the earth as well as working closely in the training and equipping of many prophets and prophetic people the last ten years, I have come to realize through experience that there are many different types of prophets and prophetic people, all according to the grace that God has given them (see Eph. 4:7). God has indeed given a measure of grace to some prophets that He has not given to others, and to try to prophesy into a sphere of influence God has not given us is dangerous and immature. In other words, all prophets and prophetic people do not have the same measure of grace from God on their lives.

I have interacted with prophets who could personally prophesy to everyone in the room but could not give a corporate prophetic word in a public meeting if they tried. I have also met so many prophets who could give a powerful corporate prophetic word during a meeting but could not personally prophesy to anyone to save their life.

I have met prophets who dream every night, and I have met prophets who never dream. I know prophets who prophesy in their local church but couldn't tell you what God is doing in their state. I know prophets who prophesy over their state but have no prophetic word for the United States. I even personally know a few prophets who are called to the nations in every sense of the word.

I've trained prophets whose sphere of influence is politics, while other prophets have grace for business, education, and media. I've equipped prophets who carry grace to prophesy to nations and their own nation. I have also had hundreds of encounters with wannabee prophets who never encountered anyone with the courage to tell them that they weren't called to be a prophet. To me, it is cruel and it does a great disservice to the prophetic movement for leaders to allow people who are not prophets or simply have the gift of prophecy to act and operate as though they are a prophet of God. Bottom line: all prophets and prophetic people do not have the same grace upon their lives, and to either compare or mimic our prophetic gifting with/to another's is foolish, discouraging, and adds unnecessary pollution and contamination to needed purified prophetic ministry.

The waters in the contemporary prophetic movement have become extremely muddied due to the fact that prophets are prophesying into spheres of influence and realms where they have no authority and anointing to do so. Much of this, I believe, is because of and in direct connection with the carnal desire of so many prophets to become "famous." In short, these prophetic messengers are filled with delusions of prophetic grandeur.

Some prophets are so desperate to build their platform and name brand that they will pretty much try to predict or attach their name to any large event, political race, or natural disaster. "I prophesied that…" they say. "I already had a dream or word about that!" they say. All at the expense of causing more confusion in the body of Christ because it appears that all the "prophets" have a "word" for everything and anything these days. Without accountability for inaccurate prophecy being given, especially on a national level, and strong correction from seasoned prophets for wandering into a sphere of influence that a prophet has no business going into, delusions of prophetic grandeur will continue to pollute and contaminate the desperately needed pure prophetic river that God wants to wash His body with.

The body of Christ and contemporary prophetic culture must be taught and understand that prophetic maturity is measured by how restrained and what degree of self-control a prophet possesses, not by whether they have a prophetic word for every event or occurrence in the earth. True prophets are not vending machines. They do not have a new prophetic word every day. If they do, it's not God talking to them! These so-called "prophets" are just trying to keep their partner base happy and giving them more money they don't really need.

Prophets and prophetic people must rid themselves of delusions of prophetic grandeur. They must fight jealousy, insecurity, and pride. This exact subject was what Paul addressed when he said in Romans 12:3, "For through the grace given to me I say to everyone among you not to think more highly of himself than he ought to think; but to think so as to have sound judgment, as God has allotted to each a measure of faith."

We must have a generation of prophets and prophetic people who do not think more highly of themselves than they ought, but who are secure in the lane God has called them to run in. When someone pressures them to speak when God hasn't spoken or come to minister when God has not sent them, they must refuse because they fear God more than they fear man.

Getting rid of delusions of prophetic grandeur and walking in a spirit of humility and brokenness would be a tremendous start to reformation within the contemporary prophetic culture and the purging, igniting, and cleansing we need. Repenting for prophetic words spoken that have never come to pass would definitely help to bring credibility back to the contemporary prophetic movement or at least open people up more to receive authentic prophetic ministry. Prophets and prophetic people operating in their metron of authority and influence and refusing to go outside of it would bring so much more accuracy and humility.

What else can be done to restore and reform authentic prophetic ministry? How can further cleansing and igniting be accomplished beyond prophets and prophetic people learning how to stay in their lane and jurisdiction? I believe the answer is found in the need to differentiate an individual who has the gift of prophecy from someone who is called to be a prophet of God. Could a major source of pollution in the contemporary prophetic movement be found in the fact that we now call people "prophets" who really just have the gift of prophecy that brings general encouragement and blessing? Let's unpack this question and get to the root of the issue in the next chapter.

# CHAPTER 5

# THE GIFT OF

# PROPHECY

I love the gift of prophecy that is available to all believers who are in Jesus Christ. I love it so much that I have spent the last ten years of my life teaching the ins and outs of the gift to communities of believers all over America and 15 nations in the earth. On average, I teach my prophetic school in more than 20 churches around the nation each year.

Writing to the Corinthian believers, Paul the apostle was very clear, "Pursue love, yet earnestly desire spiritual gifts, but especially that you may prophesy" (1 Cor. 14:1). Out of all the gifts that the Holy Spirit can bestow upon man, Paul wanted to encourage the believers at Corinth to specifically and especially pursue love and eagerly desire to prophesy. How wonderful! What made prophecy so special in the eyes of Paul you might ask? I believe the answer is revealed in the fact that the gift of prophecy brings forth divine revelation for the moment. Teaching or preaching is perhaps limited to notes or already prepared thoughts, but the gift of prophecy specifically speaks to the "now." Paul did not go out of his way to encourage the Corinthians to "above all else" pursue love and earnestly prophesy because he knew how destructive it could be in the body of Christ, but because he understood the power of edification, exhortation, and comfort being ministered in a body of believers. In fact, those who are not filled with and pursuing love are actually disqualified from prophetic ministry. A love for God and people is a prerequisite to operating in the gift of prophecy. The truth is that prophecy stirs up the anointing of God in people's minds and hearts. It has truly been a privilege and life-changing experience for me to be used by God to help instruct and activate prophetic ministry in local churches, regional gatherings, and conferences all over the world.

## LIMITATIONS OF THE GIFT OF PROPHECY

In First Corinthians 14:3 Paul specifically says that prophecy is for the edification, exhortation, and comfort of people, therefore placing boundaries and restrictions upon believers who operate in prophecy (KJV). Christians can at some point in their lifetime operate in prophecy (see 1 Cor. 14:31), but this by no means makes them a prophet of God. I believe there has been tremendous damage done and an enormous amount of pollution released into the contemporary prophetic movement and body of Christ in large part due to the erroneous teaching that because someone prophesies or has prophetic tendencies that it makes them a "prophet." Along with delusions of prophetic grandeur, this instruction and doctrine has caused the contemporary prophetic movement to become contaminated and defiled. It not only brings unnecessary confusion to that individual, but over time it creates a deception in the minds and hearts of people concerning who true prophets really are.

# THE SPIRIT BEHIND THE GIFT OF PROPHECY

As believers who operate in the prophetic anointing mentioned in First Corinthians 14, the words given must be full of edification, exhortation, and comfort or they should be thrown out. The Greek word for edification is *oikodome*, which in essence is the act of building up. As believers pursue love and eagerly desire to prophesy, they are to seek God for words of edification for their brothers and sisters in Christ. God is seeking to build up that which has been torn down and to speak life into that which is dead and dry.

The Greek word for exhortation in *paraklesis*, which means a calling near, a summoning, or a persuasive discourse. Words of exhortation have the ability to shift and bring saints into alignment with the will of God very quickly. They can also encourage those who are downcast and move those who are stagnant in their walk with Christ.

Finally, the Greek word for consolation is *paramuthis*, which means a calming and a comforting. Prophetic words of consolation bring healing, understanding, deliverance, and often inspire hope in the midst of turmoil.

# THE PROPHETIC COMPONENTS

I believe four specific gifts of the Holy Spirit—the gift of wisdom, the gift of knowledge, the gift of distinguishing of spirits, and the gift of prophecy—that are found in First Corinthians 12 comprise the DNA of the prophetic gift mentioned in First Corinthians 14. These four gifts can be ministered together or singularly depending on what the Spirit of God is revealing.

# WORDS OF WISDOM

Words of wisdom can be defined as direction, insight, and understanding into situations, circumstances, and events revealed by the Holy Spirit. In Acts 27:10, Paul operated in the gift of wisdom as he told the captain and crew on board the ship, "Men, I perceive that the voyage will certainly be with damage and great loss, not only of the cargo and the ship, but also of our lives." Paul was given a specific word of wisdom that sought to bring direction and understanding into their journey ahead. This is a prophetic word of wisdom in action given by the Holy Spirit.

Several years ago, God gave me a dream in which I met a man named "Steve Allen." In the prophetic dream, this man was in distress due to his business struggling and having to make key financial decisions for his company. God spoke to me and said that He wanted Steve to know that his business was not going to collapse. Although there was great decrease coming, he needed to hold on to his business and not sell it. I woke up from the dream and said to God, "I do not know a Steve Allen, but if I meet him, I will give him this prophetic dream of wisdom."

Sure enough, several weeks later I attended a conference and was seated by a man named "Steve Allen." As soon as I saw his nametag, I was stunned. I shared the dream with him and he wept. He said he was under great distress and was praying whether he should sell his business or not. I told him the dream and he found great comfort in it. Four years after this initial encounter with Steve Allen, I ran into him at another meeting. He ran right up to me and said, "Jeremiah, you won't believe what has taken place." He said, "I held on to my business through those tough times and the wisdom God gave you in the dream. Currently, we are now more successful than we have ever been. I needed the wisdom of God through that difficult season and God gave it to you. Thank you!"

## WORDS OF KNOWLEDGE

Words of knowledge are events, dates, times, and details about people's lives that are mysterious or secrets until revealed by the Holy Spirit. In John 4, Jesus encountered a woman at a well and surprised her by operating in a word of knowledge and telling her how many husbands she had in the past. In fact, Jesus told her that the man she was with currently wasn't her husband. Stunned, she said, "Sir, I perceive that you are a prophet." As this woman encountered Jesus that day and the word of knowledge that flowed through Him, she ran back home to invite her town to meet him. Many of them believed in Jesus all because of a word of knowledge.

I once went to a restaurant to meet with a group of ministry leaders. Our waitress that night was visibly downcast and broken. As I inquired of the Lord concerning what was wrong with her, I received a word of knowledge concerning her life. I also received a vision of a car accident in her past that resulted in a family member's death. She had blamed herself for what had happened and was even currently struggling with suicidal thoughts. I shared with the group of ministers the word of knowledge that I had received and we began to quietly pray for our waitress. It was getting quite late and we were the last table in the entire restaurant. As the waitress gave us our check, I shared with her what God had shown me. She immediately broke down weeping and our entire group gathered around her. We began praying and prophesying hope and destiny over her life that night and broke the power of darkness off of her. She was delivered and gave her life to Jesus Christ. At this point, the manager and kitchen staff had come over to find out what was happening.

Immediately, I received several more words of knowledge concerning many of their lives. As I began to minister these words of knowledge, they too began to cry and the power of the Holy Spirit came crashing down. What was supposed to be a dinner with some ministry friends turned into salvation and deliverance for several lost people, all because of a word of knowledge.

## THE GIFT OF DISTINGUISHING SPIRITS

Believers who operate in the gift of distinguishing spirits are given intuition by the Holy Spirit to discern good and evil, gifting and calling, and also supernatural activity. In Acts 16:17, a girl was following Paul and Silas proclaiming, "These men are slaves of the Most High God, who proclaim to you a way of salvation" (NRSV). Her statements sounded accurate and encouraging, but in the next verse, Paul turned around and rebuked the spirit she was carrying and said, "I command you in the name of Jesus Christ to come out of her!" Paul was operating in the gift of distinguishing spirits because he was not fooled by her outward speech. He discerned the spirit she was operating in and cast it out.

I was once approached by a woman and her husband who were dealing with nightmares and demonic activity in their home. They said they had prayed, but nothing was working. I asked if I could visit their home and pray for them there and they agreed. As I sat at their dining room table and began to pray, my eyes were drawn to a specific cabinet in their kitchen. I asked the woman what was in the cabinet and she went ghost white and started stuttering. Her husband was visibly shaken and walked to the cabinet. He explained that it was full of wine and liquor that they enjoyed with their friends every once in a while. The Holy Spirit immediately spoke through me and said, "You are giving satan legal access into your home by hosting spirits here in your kitchen. Get rid of the spirits and they will leave you alone." I was quickly asked to leave their home and that couple was divorced within six months. The gift of distinguishing spirits can cause hidden things to come into the light very quickly.

## GIFT OF PROPHECY

The gift of prophecy is predicting the future by the Holy Spirit. Out of the four gifts of the Holy Spirit that make up the prophetic components, this is the gift that is least operated in by believers. It is very rare for a believer who is operating in prophecy to predict the future. Agabus, who was a prophet in the first-century Church, accurately predicted a coming famine to the leaders at Antioch.

We must understand that the gift of prophecy mentioned in First Corinthians 14 contains four gifts of the Holy Spirit—wisdom, knowledge, distinguishing spirits, and prophecy itself.

To be clear, believers who operate in these gifts are given specific instructions and boundaries in the New Testament. Paul did not encourage prophetic ministry at Corinth with a desire to see it bring destruction. He charged the Corinthians to seek to operate in prophecy because of the blessing and power it releases in a community of believers. Fault-finding and accusation are not gifts of the Holy Spirit and should never be welcomed as prophetic ministry. Spontaneous prophecy can be given by all believers in Jesus Christ and it must edify, exhort, and bring comfort to the hearers.

Pursuing love is the first step in the process of flowing in prophecy. As stated previously, if a Christian is not filled with love for their brother and sister in Christ, they are disqualified from operating in prophecy. If believers are condemning, accusing, and pointing the finger in the name of "the gift of prophecy," they are out of line with New Testament teaching concerning prophetic ministry and must be corrected.

While Paul encouraged all believers to pursue love and prophesy, how is the gift of prophecy different from those who are called to be prophets? Are the boundaries and restrictions placed upon believers who operate in prophecy the same for prophets of God? How can we specifically tell the difference between a believer who operates in occasional and spontaneous prophecy and a prophet who operates in consistent and revelatory prophecy? We will now look at the profile of a true prophet of God as we continue to seek divine strategy concerning how to cleanse and purify the contemporary prophetic movement of all confusion and unsettling.

# CHAPTER 6

# THE PROPHET'S
# PROFILE

I N the midst of the prophetic free-for-all and the delusions of prophetic grandeur overtaking parts of the body of Christ regarding prophetic ministry, we will now look at the Scriptures to help us determine the earmarks and characteristics of true prophets and seek to set apart the office of prophet from those who have the gift of prophecy. We begin in the first chapter of Jeremiah as God calls, consecrates, and commissions the prophet. Regarding his calling, Jeremiah 1:9-10 says:

> *Then the Lord reached out his hand and touched my mouth and said to me, "I have put my words in your mouth. See, today I appoint you over nations and kingdoms to uproot and tear down, to destroy and overthrow, to build and to plant"* (NIV).

# PROPHETS ARE NOT ALWAYS POSITIVE

It's important to note that the call on Jeremiah's life as a prophet involved four negatives and two positive aspects. On the negative side he was to uproot, tear down, destroy, and overthrow, while on the positive side he was to build and plant. Lest we think that this astounding ratio is simply limited to the Old Testament, let us look no further than the words of Paul the apostle as he commissions his son in the Lord, Timothy, on how to use the Word of God. He says in Second Timothy 4:2, "Preach the word; be prepared in season and out of season; correct, rebuke and encourage—with great patience and careful instruction" (NIV). In teaching the Word of God, Paul instructs Timothy to correct, rebuke, and encourage. This is a two-to-one ratio of negative to positive. In Jeremiah 1 it is a four-to-two ratio. In verse 3, Paul sharply warns Timothy of the days ahead: "For the time will come when they will not endure sound doctrine; but wanting to have their ears tickled, they will accumulate for themselves teachers in accordance to their own desires."

After briefly looking at the call of Jeremiah the prophet in Jeremiah 1 and the four-to-two ratio God commissioned him into as well as Paul's instructions to Timothy of the two-to-one ratio, how have we limited the prophet's ministry to pure encouragement in the body of Christ? Furthermore, how have we created false paradigms where any type of messenger—apostles, teachers, pastors, and evangelists—can no longer rebuke and correct the body of Christ with the Word of God? This practice is not only unbiblical but is the very thing Paul warned would happen in future days.

I believe that the body of Christ in many ways rejects true prophets who have the capacity to tear down and uproot merely because we have been conditioned to believe that every time we attend church we should expect to leave feeling better about ourselves or something is wrong.

It is truly heartbreaking to hear and see how quickly church leaders and saints reject any sermons, or even prophetic words from prophets, that tear down, uproot, overthrow, rebuke, and correct practices out of line with the Word of God. They shout, "That's Old Testament! Get to the encouragement, building, and planting." But Paul is very clear in his instructions to Timothy that anyone who has been called to preach the Word of God, regardless of whether they are even a prophet or not, has been called to rebuke, correct, and encourage the body of Christ.

So the first thing we must understand about a prophet's profile is that they are not limited to simply encouraging the body of Christ. They actually have a mandate and an assignment that will be very confrontational at times. Their words will often bring necessary rebuke and correction and should always be given in brokenness and with humility. A.W. Tozer understood this when he wrote and said:

> The words of true prophets are not harsh for the sake of being harsh; they speak words necessary for God to finish His work. God cannot build until He tears down. He cannot plant until He roots up the evil and self-seeking ways of men. He cannot and will not sully His ways with the methods of men; the overlooking of sin to populate their churches and accomplish their agendas. He must tear down the lofty pursuits of those who seek the preeminence in His house.[1]

# THE TRAINING OF PROPHETS

Receiving the capacity as prophets of God to minister prophetic words that correct, rebuke, uproot, and tear down is no small matter in the sight of God. In fact, this calling is so sacred to the heart of God that it becomes much easier to recognize who has a true calling to be a prophet and who does not by how these types of words are delivered to people. True prophets of God will never deliver weighty and corrective words of prophecy without agony and at times with much weeping and prayer. A true prophet will continually find him/herself caught in the tension of standing before a holy God and yet called to minister to sinful man. True prophets cringe at, but must embrace at times, their assignment as one that calls them to turn the people back to God through cries for repentance, holiness, and returning to their first love.

Those in the body of Christ who have been given the gift of prophecy have limitations placed upon them per First Corinthians 14. The prophetic words they deliver must be full of encouragement, comfort, and strength. However, and as mentioned above, true prophets will not only follow the guidelines mentioned in First Corinthians 14, but they have also been given permission and capacity to uproot, tear down, overthrow, and destroy when necessary.

Will prophets continually and always move in this capacity? Absolutely not! In fact, if prophets only uproot and tear down and never build up and plant, they are unbalanced and dangerous. Prophets operate in a prophetic anointing where they edify, exhort, and comfort, but they may also at times uproot, tear down, destroy, and overthrow practices and belief systems that oppose the Word of God.

# PROPHETIC JURISDICTION

Why do those who hold prophetic office have this jurisdiction that saints with the gift of prophecy do not have? The answer is simple: The process and training that God puts true prophets through is entirely different because He has entrusted them with a weightier and deeper call upon their life. Many prophets go through severe trial and testing, not because of sin in their life but because of the prophetic call on their life. In order for cleansing and purification to come to the contemporary prophetic movement, true prophets themselves will have to be cleansed and purged. While saints may have a gift of prophecy, prophets themselves are the gift to the body of Christ. Their calling is not only to deliver the message God has given them, but with time and maturity they will become the message God has given them and it will carry a very high cost and involve much pain and suffering. Simply put, the price that true prophets will pay to operate in their calling versus those who have the spontaneous and occasional gift of prophecy is entirely and visibly different.

# WILDERNESS TRAINING

The primary difference between those who have been called as prophets of God and those who carry the gift of prophecy is found in whether or not they have been trained in the wilderness.

The wilderness is the training ground for every true prophet of God. It destroys fleshly ambition. It wrecks the need to be seen. It teaches humility in ways that none of us can teach ourselves, destroying every fleshly confidence in self until nothing remains but a purified hunger for the Lord Himself.

It is in the wilderness where authentic prophets find their voice. They learn how to die to pride and arrogance and become dependent upon God for everything. Taking up the cross and following Jesus is center stage in the wilderness.

The training and development of true prophets of God is so thorough and intense that anyone who actually desires to be a prophet is either ignorant of the wilderness seasons of preparation or simply believes they hold the office of prophet, but in truth they do not. True prophets of God walk with a limp. True prophets don't even necessarily desire to be prophets. They understand the cost involved in their calling. True prophets have the scars to prove the authority they walk in as they have paid a steep price that few understand or will ever recognize.

## THE TENSION PROPHETS LIVE IN

Listen now to the agony that Jeremiah the prophet experienced as he stated these words to the Lord concerning his divine prophetic calling,

> *O Lord, You have deceived me and I was deceived. You have overcome me and prevailed. ...If I say, "I will not remember Him or speak anymore in His name," then in my heart it becomes like a burning fire...I cannot endure it* (Jeremiah 20:7,9).

The call on Jeremiah the prophet was so difficult that he began to say to God, "You tricked me! You deceived me! I can't get away from You. Every time I try and busy myself with other things, Your word becomes like a fire in my bones. God, I don't want to deliver these hard words. It's Your fault! You put me up to this" (my paraphrase).

Yes, true prophets carry weighty words full of revelation, correction, and direction, but this is a sacred trust they have been given by God Himself because of the difficult training they have endured. True prophets never enjoy or look forward to delivering correction and rebuke. Supposed "prophets" who release heavy-handed words without brokenness and the heart of the Father have clearly not been through the wilderness training that true prophets go through.

If the contemporary prophetic movement is to be cleansed and purified, we must see the emergence of true prophets in the body of Christ who are received and embraced. Yes, they will build and yes they will plant, but they also fulfill their mandate by tearing down, uprooting, overthrowing, and destroying. We cannot throw them away or dismiss these true prophets any longer just because they carry the capacity to disrupt and challenge accepted religious practices and traditions of men.

## TWO PROPHETIC COMPANIES

Two very distinct companies are emerging from within the contemporary prophetic movement. The first company is what I call the "politically correct company." This group is fueled by an embrace of spontaneous prophecy that is purely encouraging, uplifting, and "feel good." This style of prophecy thrives on telling people what they want to hear. Any prophetic words of warning, rebuke, or correction are categorically rejected by those in this prophetic camp. The goal of politically correct prophecy is to keep everyone happy and believing that God is in a good mood all the time.

I call the second emerging company the "prophetically correct" company. While this prophetic company embraces spontaneous prophecy, they also welcome and receive revelatory prophetic words that root out, pull down, destroy, and overthrow. What the politically correct camp calls "critical," the prophetically correct camp calls "biblical." The goal of the prophetically correct camp is to deliver the word and heart of the Lord, whether the people like it or not. One of the core issues that separates these two prophetic companies is whether prophets have the capacity and permission to uproot, tear down, destroy, and overthrow, or must they keep their words and ministry positive all the time?

I firmly believe that the *gift* of prophecy, as opposed to the actual call of a prophet, has become so exalted and elevated in the contemporary prophetic movement—and overall prophetic ministry so watered down—that the body of Christ can hardly even recognize authentic prophets anymore. We do not know how to rejoice and celebrate true prophets and the nature of the call on their lives. In order for the contemporary prophetic movement to be cleansed and ignited, we are going to have to start welcoming and embracing the true prophets who are graced not only to build and plant, but to correct, rebuke, tear down, and overthrow. Yes, all of this must be done with humility, tears, and wilderness training, but nonetheless, the true prophets cannot be pacified and shut out any longer. The purifying and cleansing of the contemporary prophetic movement depends upon it!

# CHAPTER 7

# MY PROPHETIC

# JOURNEY

**W**HEN I was in my mother's womb, she had a prophetic dream one night in which God came to her and said to name me "Jeremiah" and that I was called as a prophet to the nations. God said that there would be great complications that would mark my entrance into the world and in the delivery room. That prophetic word quickly came to pass. I was born three weeks late at ten pounds, and with the umbilical cord wrapped around my neck several times. I wasn't breathing. The doctors miraculously not only saved me, but my mother as well. It was apparent to both of my parents from an early age that God had divine plans for me.

I had the privilege of growing up in a charismatic church that my father pastored. I was raised in a supernatural environment where the prophetic, miracles, and the five-fold ministry were all welcomed and embraced. I remember giving my first corporate prophetic word at nine years old and prophetically dreaming on a weekly basis shortly after that. Growing up in this type of environment, I assumed that everyone could hear from God and that was the end of it. Sadly, I was mistaken.

As a teenager, my father would constantly take us to various prophetic and prayer conferences all throughout the United States. I received over 100 recorded prophecies by the time I graduated high school.

At 18 I headed to Bible college, where I quickly found myself among other pastor and missionary kids who knew about God but did not know Him in a personal way. I barely survived in that religious environment for those two years before my life was radically changed forever. My parents decided to separate and eventually divorce. It was the most difficult experience of my life at the time. My whole world was torn apart, and I did not know what to do. After some prayer, I decided to move back home with my dad to be closer to my three brothers and mother.

In search of answers and perspective, I decided to work in a box factory from 4:00 a.m. to 4:00 p.m., Monday to Friday, with my father who had now stepped down from ministry. Those days were extremely difficult, to say the least. Growing up in a pastor's home and then leaving for Bible college to pursue ministry, God used those days in the factory to humble me, test me, and, honestly, to crush me. It was humiliating to my flesh, while at the same time I grew more in the Spirit than ever before. I was hungry for God and believed that this time away from Bible college and with my family was part of my prophetic development. I was becoming convinced that I had paid my dues and that God was going to release me back to school. Boy, was I wrong!

As I began to wrestle with God one winter morning in the factory, I cried out and said, "God, I know there is a call on my life. You spoke to my mom when I was in her womb. I can hear Your voice and I want to share Your heart and words with people. I have obeyed You by taking a break from Bible college and let You pretty much crush me. I cannot take this anymore. Release me, please!"

The tears were streaming now. I was at the end of my rope. The pain and heartache of my parents' divorce and life as I had known it was over and it finally caught up with me. Out of the silence in the back of that factory, God spoke a word to me that would change my life forever. He said, "Jeremiah, I love you and I want you to know that there is a greater crucifixion for your soul that I have prepared for you."

I was so stunned by what I had heard that I began to bind up the devil and what the Lord had just whispered to me in my brokenness. Surely, that couldn't be God! I heard the voice again, "Jeremiah, I love you and there is a greater crucifixion for your soul that awaits you. The pain and suffering that you have now and will go through in the future is not because of the sin in your life but because of the call on your life. I am sending you to India to work with lepers."

That's all I heard and that's all I wanted to hear. I didn't eat for two days, I was so disturbed. I went back to my house after work and opened up my Bible. As I searched and asked God "why," He revealed to me a place called the wilderness that I not only was in currently, but that He calls every one of His servants the prophets into, including His very own Son Jesus Christ.

## ADVENTURES TO INDIA

About a month later, I left everything that I knew and loved and found myself living north of New Delhi, India for a period of three months. For me, it was hell on earth. I lost 35 pounds, was stripped of everything comfortable and convenient, and became more on fire for God than I had ever dreamed. Boldness and courage came upon me day after day as I learned how to die daily. I finally realized that power comes from crushing and life comes from death. It was only as I learned how to fellowship in the sufferings of Christ that I could also partake in His resurrection.

# CRUCIFYING THE FLESH

In hindsight, God sent me home to Indiana to work in that factory to humble me, test me, and strip me of my pride and arrogance. All because He loved me. Then He sent me to India with a plan to kill more of my flesh, all for His glory. It was very painful and it was incredibly glorious. The voice of God became clearer to me than ever before. I fellowshipped and walked with Him on a deeper level than I had ever known. I had thoughts of perhaps remaining a missionary or even traveling the world, preaching the gospel and making disciples.

At the end of three months of living in India, I had the same prophetic dream three nights in a row. In the dream, I saw my Bible college campus on fire and God said to me, "I am sending you back in the spirit of John the Baptist for a student awakening." After waking up from the prophetic dream on the third night, I started to sob. I cried out and said, "God, I can't go back! They won't even recognize me anymore. You have crushed me, humiliated me, and worked Your character inside of me. What will my friends think?" I didn't hear a thing.

I said, "God, but I don't have any money for school. How will I make it in?" Still I heard nothing, but I didn't need to. God had spoken very clearly to me and I knew I must be obedient.

# BACK TO SCHOOL

It was the month of August when I arrived back on campus and headed straight for the registrar's office. I explained who I was and the two years that I had completed of school. I told them that I had gone home to work and then ended up in India for a season. The woman did not seem to care. After going through my files, she looked at me and said, "I'm sorry. You do not have any financial aid available and it's impossible to sign you up for classes." I was stunned. How could this be?

How could God call me to go back home and work in a box factory, live in India, and endure so much pain and suffering all because of the prophetic call on my life? I didn't know what else to do but fast and pray. I knew God would answer me.

# DIVINE PROVISION

Within one week, I was introduced to an older woman who asked me to share my life story with her. I started from my supernatural birth experience all the way to the present. She sat, listened, and even cried with me. At the end of our time together, she stepped forward and changed my destiny forever. She kindly offered to pay for my school until I graduated. A sum that eventually added up to over 50 thousand dollars!

To say I was shocked would be an understatement. I arrived back on campus wearing an Indian tunic I had from my time in India and started hosting all-night prayer gatherings. I began to teach on the prophetic ministry to anyone who would listen, and God began to move in unprecedented ways. I began attending as many prophetic conferences as I could and even hitchhiked across the United States to sit under the teaching of prophets whom I respected.

Pastors' kids and missionaries' kids at the Bible college who grew up in the church singing songs and quoting Scriptures without ever really knowing God in an intimate way began radically encountering Jesus for the very first time. We traveled on the road to Emmaus together. It was incredible. I eventually got a job working as a college pastor for the remainder of my schooling until I met and married my wife. During that season, we established a college ministry of more than 250 students, and many of the prayer and worship gatherings would last until three in the morning. We saw radical conversions on the streets, demonic deliverance, and prophetic destiny spoken on a weekly basis.

# A RADICAL ENCOUNTER

As God was moving powerfully in the college ministry my wife and I had planted, we decided to take a group of students to a prophetic conference to hear and encounter God. At the opening night of the session, I had an experience that totally took me by surprise. I received an open vision where God told me I was going to plant a church.

Never in a million years would I have guessed that after graduating Bible college God would ask me to plant a church! Me? A prophet? I wasn't a pastor! When we returned from the prophetic conference, I met with the pastor of the church where I was working to share what had happened. I told him that I believed the vision was futuristic, but wanted to have him father and help me along the way. I believed this was the appropriate course to take.

# REJECTED AND FALSELY ACCUSED

Without warning or hesitation, the pastor said to me at the meeting, "Jeremiah, if you want to plant a church now or ever within 50 miles of here, you are fired right now. I'll give you 24 hours to think about it."

I immediately walked out of the church bawling my eyes out. I called my wife and couldn't even get the words out. I was in total shock. I didn't eat a bite of food for the next 24 hours. I had been given a very sobering ultimatum from my pastor. Either I totally deny and forget that God called me to plant a church or just keep leading the college ministry.

I knew I couldn't deny the experience that I had, so the next day I met with the pastor and board and told them I knew that God had called me to plant a church, but it wasn't until a few years later. Couldn't they work with me and help father me along the way? They refused and fired me on the spot. As a newlywed and recent Bible college graduate, I was completely devastated. The next day I received an even more painful phone call—the denomination I was licensed with planned a meeting where they were going to revoke my credentials as false accusations began to emerge. I couldn't believe it. They were saying I was a "false prophet."

I drove to the meeting the next day in total silence. I called my dad in the parking lot and told him I just couldn't go in. "Why me, Dad?" I cried. "I'm just trying to fulfill the call of God and I'm being totally rejected and falsely accused."

I'll never forget his words. "Son, you need this as part of your destiny. You must understand the sting of rejection and false accusation so that you never operate in this spirit and so that you will learn to father many gifted leaders rather than allowing your insecurities to reject them."

I walked into the meeting with the denomination and was stripped of my credentials. They rebuked me and falsely accused me for two hours. God told me to remain silent the entire time. Although I was like a lamb led to the slaughter, I felt the Holy Spirit begin to minister to deep places in my heart like never before.

# PLANTING THE CHURCH

Without a job and still reeling from the pain and rejection, I cried out to God the following week and asked Him what to do. He first told me He wanted me to put the pastor's picture on our fridge who had rejected me and to pray for him and his family every day. He would deliver me from all bitterness and forgiveness, and He did too! He then said, "Fulfill the vision I have given you to plant the church."

So at 22 years old, we planted the church and began having prayer and Bible study meetings in our home. God spoke to my heart so clearly in that season and said, "Jeremiah, I love you and I have called you as a prophetic shepherd of My people. The days of lone ranger prophetic ministry are over. I will teach you not only to prophesy and preach My fire, but to love My people and embrace their brokenness and pain."

We recently celebrated our eight-year anniversary as "Heart of the Father Ministry" in Lakeland, Florida, and it truly is by God's grace that we are thriving and witnessing God pouring out His Spirit in tremendous ways. From our living room with no money and a handful of people to now owning a multi-million dollar facility with hundreds of quality people and an incredible staff, I find myself continually in awe of all that God has done.

The early years of our church plant were not easy. As a prophet of the Lord, God used the early days as a true tester of my heart attitudes and motives. If I could learn how to shepherd the people of God and love them through their brokenness, I was convinced and still am that anyone can.

## SEARCHING FOR A PROPHETIC FATHER

Although I grew up with parents who mentored me in the prophetic gifts God had given me, I always found myself hungry to mature and learn more. In search of a greater realm of fathering in the prophetic, I read an article online one day by a man named R. Loren Sandford. It was as if he was communicating my heart regarding prophetic ministry better than I could. Without thinking, I emailed him and asked if he took appointments. He did, but the problem was I didn't have any money, so I prayed and asked God for the funds. The next day, a man walked up to me and handed me 500 dollars cash and told me God said to sow it into my life, so he was obedient.

The next day I spontaneously flew out to Denver, Colorado to meet with R. Loren Sandford, this man I had never heard or met before. All I knew was that I was hungry for prophetic fathering and was willing to pay any price to mature and go deeper.

My time in Denver with Loren was life changing to say the least. I have now walked with him closely for more than five years and it has been one of the greatest blessings of my life. He has faithfully rebuked me, corrected me, and encouraged me. We have walked as a father and son in the prophetic and it all started with hunger. God is looking for a company of prophets and prophetic people who are hungry to be fathered and mature in their gifts and calling.

# GOD CALLS ME TO REPENT

During my journey as a church planter and maturing in the prophetic call upon my life, I felt strongly compelled one day by the Spirit of God to write an open letter of apology to the body of Christ for any way that I might have offended or caused anyone harm in my journey to learn how to mature and develop as a prophet in the midst of what God had and has called me to do. I have no desire to hide the mistakes I have made on my prophetic journey. I hope that others can learn and grow from where I have failed. I have included the letter I wrote several years ago in hope that my transparency will be an encouragement to the reader.

## LETTER OF REPENTANCE TO BODY OF CHRIST

Greetings,

At the leading of the Holy Spirit, I would like to officially issue a public statement of repentance to all those that I have offended or hurt with my public ministry over the last ten years. I have recently come to the realization and for me personally, a revelation, of how at times I might have ministered the word of the Lord without the Father's heart. There have been moments where perhaps I was too hard with my words on the bride of Christ and failed to properly and maturely communicate what I have received from the Father in a way that truly pleases Him.

I was recently invited to minister prophetically at a retreat where pastors and their wives had gathered for a time of impartation and refreshing. We had a tremendous time in God's presence and I taught and prophesied over each couple. As I was leaving that day, the man who invited me to the event stopped me as I was getting in my car and said, "One thing I am learning is that Jesus said, 'I am the way, the truth, and the life.' He didn't say, 'I am the way, the truth, and I'M RIGHT.'"

I am not sure what prompted that precious brother to say that to me, but all I can say is that an arrow was shot straight out of heaven that pierced my heart in that moment and has wounded me in a way that I do not have adequate words to describe. On my drive home as I wept in my car, God the Father spoke to me and said, *"When are you finally going to lay down your need to be right prophetically and start releasing life like the father I have called you to be in the body of Christ?"* That one question from the Father caused me to do some sobering heart and motive searching.

The Holy Spirit began to show me that as I labored to establish the church plant in the early years, I somewhere along the way drifted from the Father's heart and at times began preaching out of my own frustration and not the place of revelation. Perhaps at times, I even drove out people from our midst in Lakeland who were the very people God was sending in an attempt to tenderize and soften my young prophetic heart. I was carrying the capacity as a young prophet to clearly see where God wanted to take our community, but I was unable to communicate the vision with a father's heart. I was impatient and desiring to get us to our destiny way too fast and did not have enough compassion for those who were struggling.

For my insensitivity to the brokenness of humanity, for my inability to bend down and bear the burdens of the hurting, for my zeal without wisdom, and my hastiness in driving the saints rather than releasing them to the Father, I publicly repent to "Heart of the Father Ministry" and the public for my mistakes, which I will have to stand before God and be held accountable for. I sincerely apologize for any hurt or misrepresentation of the Father's heart that I have brought to anyone's life because of my words or actions. I am sorry that my need to be right and prove my point prophetically failed to release life in our community and the world around me. I am now committed more than ever to practically and with tenderness release life as a father to all those who are in need. I will bring the word of the Lord with the Father's heart in the days ahead. Please forgive me.

It is my hope and prayer that by sharing this letter, many of you who have picked up this book would be prompted by the Holy Spirit to examine and evaluate the prophetic ministry God has given you, whether you are a believer who operates in the gift of prophecy or one who is called to be a prophet of God. We are all on our own journey to mature and grow in the gifts God has given us and we must seek to walk humbly in them, repenting and asking forgiveness wherever we might have failed God and others. Many of us have faced rejection, family betrayal, wounding from the Church and church leaders, and it's time to heal and forgive.

I believe the cleansing and igniting of the contemporary prophetic movement will come as we each search our own hearts and pray as David prayed in Psalm 139:23-24, "Search me, oh God, and know my heart...and see if there be any hurtful way in me, and lead me in the everlasting way." Can I encourage you to take a few minutes right now and put this book down? Ask God to search your own heart and give you perspective concerning your own prophetic journey and seasons of development? We all have made mistakes, but owning them and repenting for them will bring healing and restoration to our lives and many others in the process. We all have been rejected and hurt in some way, but choosing to forgive is a more excellent way. It's much easier to point out what's wrong with the Church and people than actually be part of the solution and answer. Take some time to pray now and ask God to reveal His heart for you in this moment.

# CHAPTER 8

# THE HYPER-GRACE PROPHETIC
# MOVEMENT

I believe the greatest threat and danger to the desperately needed cleansing and igniting of the contemporary prophetic movement is the rise of what I call the "hyper-grace prophetic movement." One of the most common teachings of the hyper-grace movement is that the Holy Spirit does not convict believers of sin. In some circles, modern grace teachers are now claiming that the Holy Spirit does not even convict unsaved sinners of their sin. How have these beliefs infiltrated the contemporary prophetic movement? Very simply, the emergence of a hyper-grace prophetic movement led by hyper-grace prophets is upon us. It must be exposed if we are going to see sanctified prophetic ministry today.

Hyper-grace prophets teach that in the New Testament Church there is no room for the judgment of God. They say that prophetic words of correction and rebuke are no longer acceptable because we are living under a New Covenant. They teach that the body of Christ is now in a prophetic season of grace because God judged Jesus on the Cross. The hyper-grace prophetic movement categorically rejects prophetic words that call out specific sin, demand repentance, bring correction, and release rebuke.

The hyper-grace prophetic movement loves spontaneous words of prophecy full of general encouragement and blessing. They welcome them with open arms. In a book I co-authored with R. Loren Sandford called *The Micaiah Company: A Prophetic Reformation*, I wrote concerning two types of prophecy—spontaneous prophecy and revelatory prophecy.

## THEY LOVE SPONTANEOUS AND GENERAL PROPHECY

The hyper-grace prophetic movement is built upon spontaneous and general prophecy. As I have written in a previous chapter, and will reiterate here now for the sake of continued clarification, all believers are capable of prophesying on a spontaneous level, particularly in a small group setting and even in worship.

Paul addresses this gift in First Corinthians 14:1-5. The saints can bring edification, exhortation, and comfort to the body of Christ on many levels. It is necessary and extremely beneficial among believers. Crisis and tension come in when the only form of acceptable prophecy is spontaneous prophecy. What about revelatory prophecy? All believers are capable of operating in spontaneous prophecy, but only those called to be prophets of God have the grace and training to operate in revelatory prophecy.

One of the primary mistakes the hyper-grace prophetic movement has made is that they have exalted believers who operate in general and spontaneous prophecy to the place of being labeled as prophets of

God and therefore have misled an entire generation of believers and caused them to reject revelatory prophecy.

## REVELATORY PROPHECY

One of the distinct earmarks of revelatory prophecy is that it carries weight and authority in the spirit realm because it is typically born in the place of prayer and fasting. Revelatory prophecy has the capacity to shift and change seasons in the body of Christ. It often requires days, weeks, and months of meditation and inquiring of the Lord before it is publicly released. Revelatory prophecy often calls for repentance and warns of consequences and coming judgments of God if the word of the Lord is ignored. Revelatory prophecy is granted to prophets alone. Prophets have been given permission and granted the capacity to carry weighty and heaven-shaking prophetic words from the Lord that can change an entire generation. The hyper-grace prophetic movement has no frame of reference for this.

## HAS THE NEW COVENANT CHANGED PROPHECY?

We must now look intently into the Scriptures to decide for ourselves whether we believe and agree with the hyper-grace prophetic movement and their prophets when they say that God no longer releases prophets to rebuke, correct, uproot, and tear down. Do we believe that spontaneous and general prophetic words of encouragement and blessing are the only acceptable forms of prophecy now that we are under a New Covenant and Jesus has died on the Cross? Was Jesus really the first of a new breed of prophets under the New

Covenant who would no longer bring words of repentance, warning, correction, and judgment? Did Jesus simply have a prophetic ministry of encouragement that never called people out on their sin and focused on making people feel better about themselves every time they attended one of His meetings?

## JESUS PROPHESIES

Let's begin in the book of Revelation after Jesus has already died and rose again. Seven letters are written to seven different churches in Asia Minor, and we find that Jesus Himself rebuked five out of the seven churches. The reasons for the rebukes vary, but it is certainly noteworthy that only two of the seven churches found themselves receiving encouragement and blessing from Jesus. In Revelation 3:19, Jesus says to the church in Laodicea, "Those whom I love, I reprove and discipline; therefore be zealous and repent." This word "discipline" is the same Greek word for "judgment" that Paul used concerning the Corinthians whom God judged (disciplined) because of the inappropriate way they partook of the Lord's supper (see 1 Cor. 11:29-32). In this context, then, to the church at Laodicea Jesus says, "Those whom I love, I rebuke and judge, so be zealous and repent."

The words of Jesus Christ here in Revelation 3:19 clearly do not agree with the hyper-grace prophetic movement in any form or fashion. The hyper-grace prophetic movement claims that because Jesus died on the Cross, there is now no more room for rebuke or judgment on believers. According to His words to the Laodicean church, that statement could not be any more deceptive and incorrect. According to Jesus, loving His Church includes rebuking and redemptively judging them. Calling them to repentance because of their sin is pure love in the eyes of Jesus Christ.

# IS GOD IN A GOOD MOOD ALL THE TIME?

The hyper-grace prophetic movement teaches that Jesus is always in a good mood. He isn't ever angry or upset with anyone, and because of this only words of encouragement and blessing can be spoken over people's lives. But here again, as Jesus is addressing the seven churches in Asia Minor, He says to the church at Sardis, "Wake up! Strengthen what remains and is about to die, for I have found your deeds unfinished" (Rev. 3:2 NIV). That does not sound encouraging to me! Jesus is not telling everyone in Sardis that they get an "A" for trying. He says, "I have found your works incomplete." In other words, Jesus looked upon His church and called their sin out. He called them to wake up and repent. How do the words of Jesus in the book of Revelation to His seven churches agree with the teachings of the hyper-grace prophetic movement? The simple answer is they don't. The words of Jesus Himself after His death and resurrection contradict the current teachings of hyper-grace prophets telling the body of Christ that words of correction and judgment are no longer valid now that we are in a season of "grace" because of His sacrifice.

# WE CAN'T CHERRY PICK

The hyper-grace prophetic movement thrives on cherry-picking Scripture. What this means is that they pick and choose what they want to quote and not quote to back up their belief systems. For example, John 3:16 says "For God so loved the world, that He gave His only begotten Son, that whoever believes in Him shall not perish, but have eternal life." This is the greatest news ever declared to humanity. All those who choose to believe in Jesus will not perish but have eternal life.

What then is the status of those who refuse to believe in Jesus? Twenty verses later in verse 36 this question is answered: "He who believes in the Son has eternal life; but he who does not obey the Son will not see life, but the wrath of God abides on him." A further study into the Greek language will show that the wrath of God is currently and continually abiding upon all those who do not believe in Jesus Christ. The hyper-grace prophetic movement will only support and emphasize the God of John 3:16, but will not make known the God of John 3:36.

Another example of this is revealed when the hyper-grace prophets declare Romans 2:4, that the "kindness of God leads you to repentance," but will not mention the next verse, which says, "But because of your stubbornness and unrepentant heart you are storing up wrath for yourself in the day of wrath and revelation of the righteous judgment of God." The hyper-grace prophetic movement will never be faithful to warn unbelievers that the wrath of God is not only currently and continually abiding upon them, but it is also being stored up for them on the day of judgment. They will only tell people about the love and kindness of God. They will keep all prophetic ministry general and encouraging; by doing so, at worst they will lead astray millions of souls into hell, and at best they completely misrepresent who Jesus really is to this generation.

# THE SPIRIT OF PROPHECY

Revelation 19:10 says that "the testimony of Jesus is the spirit of prophecy." In other words, prophetic ministry must rightly represent all of who Jesus really is. Under the New Covenant, because He loves them, Jesus still rebukes, corrects, and disciplines those who believe in Him. In extreme cases, Jesus even struck down Ananias and Sapphira for their sin as believers. What was the fruit of God in bringing judgment upon the first-century Church in the book of Acts?

1. *"Great fear seized the whole church and all who heard about these events"* (Acts 5:11 NIV).

2. Unusual respect and honor came from outsiders toward believers. The Jews actually regarded them too highly to join them (Acts 5:13).

3. The fruit of God striking down Ananias and Sapphira as believers was that, "more and more men and women believed in the Lord and were added to their number" (Acts 5:14 NIV).

4. Power was released to the Church as people brought the sick into the streets and hoped that Peter's shadow might fall on them (Acts 5:15-16).

What tremendous fruit was birthed in the Church all because of the judgment of God!

Therefore, prophetic ministry under the New Covenant still has the capacity to rebuke, correct, and discipline. Does it need to be done with brokenness and the right heart? Absolutely! But for the hyper-grace prophetic movement to now teach that the sacrifice of Jesus on the Cross has banned prophets from delivering prophetic words that rebuke, bring correction, discipline, and call for repentance is heresy. Here are five key indicators that the hyper-grace prophetic movement has overtaken a church culture or movement:

1. Warning the people that there are consequences for their sin and rebellion now gets prophets labeled as "doomsday prophets."

2. Prophetic words calling for repentance and renouncing of specific sin is labeled as "judgmental and critical."

3. If the prophetic words are not positive and encouraging, the prophet is labeled as "operating under the Old Covenant."

4. Prophets who cry out for holiness and consecration and live a lifestyle of prayer and fasting are labeled "legalistic and harsh."

5. Prophets who call out and expose false prophets and unbiblical practices are labeled "self-righteous, prideful, and rebellious."

As we look at the life and ministry of Jesus and examine the New Testament, we see that correction, rebuke, uprooting, tearing down, and discipline are a part of prophetic ministry. Yes, building, planting, and encouraging are all a part of prophetic ministry, but we must have balance! The same call that God gave Jeremiah in chapter 1 to tear down, uproot, overthrow, and destroy under the Old Covenant still holds weight under the New Covenant as demonstrated by Jesus Christ.

# THE BLOOD OF JESUS

All believers who put their faith in Jesus Christ have been spared and saved from the wrath and judgment of God that leads to eternal punishment (see Rom. 5:9). However, believers are not spared from the redemptive judgment of God that brings discipline to their lives (see Rev. 3:19 and 1 Cor. 11:29-32). As mentioned in a previous chapter, believers in Jesus Christ are to be taught the Word of God that brings rebuke, correction, and encouragement to their lives. Yes, Jesus bore the wrath of God on the Cross so that all who put their faith in Him would not face eternal judgment, but His sacrifice does not excuse or exempt us from judgment that separates the precious from the vile. It is out of the Father's great love for us that He corrects and rebukes us with His Word. It is because of the mercy and compassion of God that He endorses and releases His prophets who release words of correction and rebuke—words that uproot and tear down.

## THE ORPHAN SPIRIT

We are living in one of the most fatherless generations that has ever lived. Abuse and absenteeism among fathers has contributed to some very distorted views of who God really is among the hyper-grace prophetic movement. This cannot be more clearly seen than on the subject of "discipline." Individuals who have an orphan spirit view discipline and correction as God's rejection of them rather than as God receiving them. I believe God desires to address this orphan spirit running rampant in our generation by revealing that because He loves us, He corrects us. When God speaks correction and rebuke to His people, it is because He loves us. Receiving His chastisement is the mark that we are His (see Heb. 12).

## THE WRATH OF GOD

What about all those who do not put their faith in Jesus Christ? Is God happy and pleased with them? Should prophets tell people who are not believers that God is in a good mood and in love with them?

To the contrary, the very first message Jesus preached to unbelievers was "flee from the coming wrath" (Matt. 3:7 NIV). Paul wrote in Romans 1:18, "For the wrath of God is revealed from heaven against all ungodliness and unrighteousness of men who suppress the truth in unrighteousness."

John 3:36 says, "He who believes in the Son has eternal life; but he who does not obey the Son will not see life, but the wrath of God abides on him." The wrath of God that brings eternal judgment is currently resting upon sinners. God is not in love with sinners; He is actually repulsed with their sin. True prophets of God do not tell a generation living in wickedness and sin that God is at peace with them. Making such claims would actually make them false prophets. False prophets bring comfort and assurance to a generation living in compromise that God is in a good mood and pleased with them. The blood of Jesus is not covering a generation living in sin, and they must be warned of the eternal and present consequences of their decisions. Yes, God's love is revealed for them in the fact that He sent His Son to die on the Cross for their sins, but they must choose to put their faith in Him if they are to avoid His wrath and judgment currently abiding upon them and being stored up for them on the day of judgment.

The hyper-grace prophetic movement not only believes that New Covenant prophetic ministry cannot rebuke, correct, and tell the body of Christ that God is disciplining them, but it also does not teach, warn, or prophesy to unbelievers concerning their current state (the wrath of God abiding upon them) and their future in hell if they do not repent.

Is the hyper-grace prophetic movement in danger of damning millions of unrepentant souls to hell because all they teach and prophesy is about the love and goodness of God and not also His severity and wrath? I believe the answer is yes. Is the hyper-grace prophetic movement leading believers into compromise, deception, and complacency by teaching and prophesying that only general encouragement and words that make people feel good are acceptable because Jesus has died on the Cross and now we are living in a season of grace? I believe the answer is yes. The fruit of the hyper-grace prophetic movement is so damaging that a large portion of the body of Christ can no longer recognize true prophets of God and will ultimately reject them. Furthermore, the hyper-grace prophetic movement is not only rejecting true prophets of God, but they are rejecting God Himself.

## THE WORD OF THE LORD IS NOT MAINSTREAM

We must keep in mind that the reason why the hyper-grace prophetic movement is thriving in the earth is because what has been written in this chapter is not popular, typically does not sell books well, and does not draw large crowds. I believe what Jeremiah wrote concerning the prophetic ministry in his day could be said about portions of the contemporary prophetic movement in our day. He said, "The prophets prophesy falsely, and the priests rule on their own authority; and My people love it so!" (Jer. 5:31). In the days of Jeremiah, the people loved false prophecy, and it is the same in our day! Some parts of the body of Christ do not want to hear prophetic words that rebuke, correct, uproot, and tear down practices and doctrines that are contrary to Scripture. Unbelievers do not want to hear the Word of God and prophetic words that declare to them that the wrath of God is currently abiding upon them and that if they do not repent, they will spend eternity in hell. These biblical truths are not popular, but prophets are not called to be popular. True prophets do not take polls before they prophesy. True prophets are gripped with conviction and have a love for the truth of God's Word. If the hyper-grace prophetic movement is not exposed and confronted with urgency, prophetic ministry today is in danger of failing to become cleansed and ignited like God so desires.

From a scriptural standpoint, the true word of the Lord has rarely been found in the mainstream prophetic narrative, but has always been revealed in the minority who stood against the majority. For example, Elijah stood against 850 prophets (see 1 Kings 18), Micaiah stood against 400 prophets (see 1 Kings 22), and Jeremiah stood against Hananiah and the prophets who stole words from one another (see Jer. 23 and 28).

What makes the body of Christ believe that our popular prophetic websites, magazines, and TV programs are actually publishing and releasing the true word of the Lord? I'll answer the question—they may not be!

Are we finally ready to listen to and give voice to the lone Elijahs, Micaiahs, and Jeremiahs who are crying out in this generation, contradicting and confronting much of the mainstream prophetic narrative? I have never been more convinced than I am now that segments of the body of Christ have not been currently taught biblically nor have they embraced practically the true prophets of God in this hour.

## A PERSONAL ENCOUNTER WITH THE MAINSTREAM

Several years ago, several nationally known speakers and I were asked to prophetically speak into the greatest needs of America and the Church moving forward. Through an extended time of fasting, the Spirit of God spoke to me that I was to minister on the urgent need for God to raise up real prophets in America. Halfway through, as I spoke to several thousand people the message God had given me, great travail and weeping broke out in the crowd. The weighty fear of the Lord came crashing down in our midst, and I found myself on my knees weeping and leading a spontaneous and powerful prayer meeting of repentance. As I wept, I prophesied and said, "The prophets have dined at Jezebel's table for too long. It's time for cleansing, it's time for purifying. Forgive us, oh God."

The groans and wailing in the crowd were intensifying. You could feel a tangible shift in the atmosphere as we interceded for the prophetic movement and asked God to raise up real prophets. I myself was undone and filled with many tears. As we continued to press into what God was doing in that moment, suddenly the leadership of the conference took the microphone and the stage. They proceeded to shut down what God was doing and spent the next 30 minutes trying to apologize for what just happened. Stunned, I took my seat and wept even harder.

In that divine moment of time, an eye-opening one for me personally, I came to the startling realization of how unprepared the bride of Christ and its leaders are for the prophetic reformation that is coming to the earth.

The need for cleansing and igniting in the contemporary prophetic movement has never been greater, and we are about to witness a new breed of prophets come out of the wilderness who will confront the hyper-grace prophetic movement and popular prophetic media outlets of our day with boldness and clarity. Just because someone has a recognized brand name and social media platforms does not mean they actually carry the true word of the Lord. Two or three prophets are going to prophesy and then we are finally going to see some judging (see 1 Cor. 14:29). We are going to see an accountable, authentic, and genuine prophetic spirit return to the body of Christ. The sooner the hyper-grace prophetic movement is exposed, repentance takes place, and a clear course correction is made, the more the contemporary prophetic culture will be cleansed and ignited.

# CHAPTER 9

# UNAUTHORIZED PROPHETIC
# MINISTRY

I N some parts of the contemporary prophetic movement, there is more of a hunger to obtain power than to walk in intimacy with Jesus. Some possess more of a craving to live under the anointing than to demonstrate Christlike character. Others have more of an appetite to publicly prophesy over thousands than to privately pray to the Father in heaven. Some carry more of an obsession to chase after someone else's prophetic mantle than to giving time to discovering an individually unique divine design given by the Father alone. Still others are fueled with more of an urge to chase gold dust, feathers, and angels than to encounter the Person of Jesus Christ. All of these pursuits lead to one terrifying end: The rise of a generation of "Simons the Sorcerers" who are currently operating in illegitimate authority!

These individuals carry an appearance of walking in deep relationship with Jesus, but in reality they are collateral damage to the body of Christ. These men and women are dangerous, their motives are impure, and what they primarily pursue and emphasize causes them to live in continual dysfunction. One of the main reasons the contemporary prophetic movement is headed for shipwreck is because we are continuing to honor and give individuals positions of authority who have quit on intimacy. These prophetic individuals consistently tear down with their character what they have built with their gifting.

## THE STORY OF SIMON

The account of Simon the Sorcerer is told in Acts 8:

> *Now there was a man named Simon, who formerly was practicing magic in the city and astonishing the people of Samaria, claiming to be someone great; and they all, from smallest to greatest, were giving attention to him, saying, "This man is what is called the Great Power of God." And they were giving him attention because he had for a long time astonished them with his magic arts* (Acts 8:9-11).

Phillip began preaching the good news of the kingdom in Samaria and many men and women were baptized. Even Simon the Sorcerer himself believed and was baptized and immediately started following Phillip because he was amazed at the miracles taking place. When Peter and John heard that Samaria was receiving the word of God, they came down and began to pray that people might receive the Holy Spirit. Laying hands on the new believers, many of them began to be filled and touched by God. In Acts 8:18-24 it says:

> *Now when Simon saw that the Spirit was bestowed through the laying on of the apostles' hands, he offered them money, saying, "Give this authority to me as*

*well, so that everyone on whom I lay my hands may receive the Holy Spirit." But Peter said to him, "May your silver perish with you, because you thought you could obtain the gift of God with money! You have no part or portion in this matter, for your heart is not right before God. Therefore repent of this wickedness of yours, and pray the Lord that, if possible, the intention of your heart may be forgiven you. For I see that you are in the gall of bitterness and in the bondage of iniquity." But Simon answered and said, "Pray to the Lord for me yourselves, so that nothing of what you have said may come upon me."*

One of the keys to understanding the deception Simon the Sorcerer lived in is to identify for what he hungered. He said to Peter and John, "Give this authority to me as well." Simon's desire for a position of influence and attention was the driving force behind his request to have the apostles lay hands on him. He was quickly becoming addicted to ministry and it was becoming an idol in his life. When this deadly deception overtakes an individual, destruction is right around the corner. Simon was not interested in deep union with Jesus. He was only interested in the miracle-working power of Jesus. All activity in the kingdom of God that is not born out of intimacy is unauthorized by heaven!

Peter and John had not only walked with Jesus, but as the crowds noted in Acts 4:13 as the lame crippled beggar had been healed, "they had been with Jesus." Peter and John had waited in the Upper Room to be filled with power from on high. Simon the Sorcerer was looking for a quick impartation to launch him into ministry.

Peter responded to Simon's request and said, "May your silver perish with you, because you thought you could obtain the gift of God with money!" In other words, Simon wanted authority and power so badly that he was willing to use soulish means to obtain them. Peter continued and said, "You have no part or portion in this matter, for your heart is not right before God. Therefore repent of this wickedness of yours, and pray the Lord that, if possible, the intention of your heart may be forgiven you."

I see thousands of Christian young adults who, like Simon the Sorcerer, are hungry for the supernatural and are therefore looking for an impartation, prayer, or touch from a well-known leader in the body of Christ to launch them into their ministry. Rather than seeking intimacy with Jesus Christ and walking in true legitimate kingdom authority like Peter and John, many, just like Simon, are seeking a drive-thru experience because they are hungry for authority but aren't willing to obtain it legally through intimacy.

## EMPOWERING ILLEGITIMATE AUTHORITY

We who are prophets and church leaders have placed so much emphasis on activation and impartation in our prophetic and supernatural schools, and so little time connecting people to the character and nature of God and what Jesus is really like, that we ourselves have blessed and commissioned a generation of Simon the Sorcerers who are operating in illegitimate authority in the body of Christ. Because intimacy and deep union with Jesus Christ are no longer a focus in the prophetic movement, our horrendous levels of discernment have built stages for these Simon the Sorcerers and given them platforms. We have been incredibly gullible as leaders and therefore produced extremely gullible prophetic people.

Peter told Simon the Sorcerer that his heart was not right before God. I believe Simon's desires for power and authority were not only not pleasing to God, but I believe deep within Simon's heart was an impure motive to have the apostles' hands laid on him: He was full of jealousy!

## THE SPIRIT OF JEALOUSY

We are witnessing a mass production of parrots, echoes, and mimics in the prophetic and supernatural movements. Too many prophets are forfeiting authenticity and originality for formulas and models, even in the supernatural. A large portion of immature and young prophetic people are worshiping well-known names in the body of Christ and are hungry to have hands laid on them by these individuals. Simon the Sorcerers are signing up for their conferences, their ministry schools, and their meetings. The motive behind this crazy frenzy is not a love for Jesus but a jealously of others possessing what we do not carry and a total disregard for the need for deep union with Jesus.

The fuel behind this rapidly growing movement is the spirit of jealousy cloaked in a desire for impartation and activation. Simon did not want the Holy Spirit and power from a pure heart that can only be found in those who spend time with Jesus. He was jealous of the power and authority that Peter and John walked in out of an insecure and wicked heart.

## DEEP UNION

The igniting and cleansing that is coming to the contemporary prophetic movement will produce prophets and prophetic people who will walk in legitimate authority because of their deep union with Jesus Christ and central pursuit of His character and nature. They have been trained and raised up by prophetic fathers and mothers who saw and understood early on that God was more interested in changing them than using them. Those prophetic voices who have been ignited and cleansed will not be obsessed by or enamored of another's mantle or gifting, but simply enthralled by the invitation to come sit at the feet of Jesus.

## THE COMING DISTINCTION

There is a divine confrontation quickly approaching the contemporary prophetic movement. I see a collision between a breed of Simon the Sorcerers who are going to be exposed for the illegitimate authority that they walk in and an ignited and purified company of prophets and prophetic people who walk in true kingdom authority birthed out of intimacy. Beware of these Simon the Sorcerers. They are addicted to ministry and crave the power and anointing of God from an impure heart of jealousy and a selfish desire to be famous. Instead of carrying a living and active spirit of revelation, Simon the Sorcerer types have to borrow revelation because they have no prayer life. Simon told Peter and John in Acts 8:24, "Pray to the Lord for me yourselves, so that nothing of what you have said may come upon me." The greatest distinction between this breed of Simon the Sorcerers and the ignited and cleansed prophetic voices will be deep intimacy with Jesus that can only be birthed through deep intercession and travail. Simon the Sorcerers are looking to get launched into ministry by another's touch, but the ignited and cleansed prophetic generation is looking to grow in humility under heaven's touch. This can only be accomplished through prayer and fasting.

# CHAPTER 10

# DANGER IN SUPERNATURAL PROPHETIC
# EVANGELISM

FOR many years, I was personally involved with numerous prophetic/ supernatural schools and churches from around the USA who would weekly go out to do prophetic and supernatural evangelism in different cities and regions. I can honestly say that the first ten years were incredible and nothing less than exhilarating. I was dedicated! Watching people encounter the love of God for the very first time is amazing. We saw too many physical healings, demons being cast out, and powerful words of knowledge go forth to count. From setting up "free spiritual reading" tents to simply handing out bottles of water and asking people if we could pray with them to try to lure them in for a supernatural encounter with God, I have both experienced and led many teams, and seen a lot!

However, at about the ten-year mark of walking in this realm on a consistent basis, I believe God began to open up my eyes to great danger concerning what I was doing, and what I am about to share I still consistently see and hear across the country today. *It deeply breaks my heart!* My hope in sharing what was revealed to me is to help those going out to do supernatural evangelism and even those teaching it to make some course adjustments and seek the Lord personally on these matters. Again, this chapter is to better equip those going out to do supernatural and prophetic evangelism, not discourage them from going out!

Here are four areas of danger that were revealed to me by the Holy Spirit concerning what I was doing and teaching in the supernatural/ prophetic evangelism realm:

# 1. THE GIFTS OF THE HOLY SPIRIT

As I took a hard look at the role of the gifts of the Holy Spirit in the New Testament, I was shocked at what I found. The gifts of the Holy Spirit were only used for two purposes—one was in a community and relational context among saints to promote unity and help them draw near to the presence of God, and the second was in an evangelistic setting to draw saints *into* community. In other words, to demonstrate the gifts of the Holy Spirit on the streets without intending to bring people into community and relationship with the body of Christ is unbiblical and can be misleading.

And to take it a step further, 75 percent of the people whom I did supernatural evangelism with for many years did not attend a local church faithfully and knew nothing of Christian community living. Therefore, it is dangerous to demonstrate the supernatural to the world without clearly trying to draw them into a community setting where relationship and unity can be formed. If you are going out trying to win souls, prophesy to people, and lay hands on them for healing without strongly encouraging and providing them with the correct avenues to get plugged into a community of believers where strong discipleship is taking place, I ask you to repent and turn from this deception.

## 2. HEALING AND PROPHETIC SHOWMANSHIP

I cannot count on how many occasions I have seen people healed and prophetic words given without a presentation of the gospel that includes asking people to repent of their sins. I have personally (which I have now repented of) and also taken teams all over the USA where we laid hands on the sick and crippled and saw them healed as we talked to them about the love of God and the work of the Cross, but yet never told them that they had to repent of their sins and live a consecrated life unto the Lord. It's almost like we developed a culture where people were addicted to prophesying and healing the sick and "demonstrating the love of God," but got more of a kick out of watching people encounter God than leading them to Christ. (I hope that makes sense.)

Over the years among many of us who were "gifted," it became like a game. Who could prophesy the most accurate, in-depth word or who could get the best healing? Please, if you are reading this, take this seriously. I will not name the supernatural schools or leaders, but this type of thinking is so rampant it would make you sick. Healings and prophecies and the love of God without a mention of holiness, righteous living, or the need to repent of sins. It produces people who are seeking an outward touch but reject inward transformation. They want goosebumps and stimulation but run from trials and testing. If you are praying for healing and prophesy to people, but yet not preaching the gospel by telling them that they must die to their flesh and pick up their cross and follow Jesus, I ask you to repent and turn from this deception.

# 3. WORSHIPING MIRACLES OR THE GOD OF MIRACLES?

Another area of deception that God showed me I was walking in was my obsession with the miraculous outside of a true obsession with Jesus Christ. I found myself more eager to pray and release miracles than I was to pray to the God of miracles. I began to point people more to miracle power than the God of miracle power. Even in my language and speech, I had little to no revelation of the person of God, yet I had no problem "demonstrating" His works.

It all culminated for me when I went to sleep one night and was taken to hell by the Holy Spirit. There He showed me not only miracle workers who went to hell because they never knew the Lord, but he showed me thousands of people who had received His miracle-working power when they lived yet had never truly given their heart and life to Him. If you are addicted to miracles and the prophetic and do not possess a true obsession with Jesus Christ, I ask you to repent and turn from this deception.

# 4. PROPHETIC ACTIVATION AND IMPARTATION

Probably the strongest area of deception that I walked in was the zeal to activate and impart to people the prophetic anointing without spending any time teaching them about the character and nature of God or the need for their own character transformation. I was or they were so eager to lay hands or have hands laid on them to show them how to do the "stuff" that holding their feet to the fire regarding their own sin and lack of revelation of who God is was never addressed.

I realized over the years that I was actually launching collateral damage rather than releasing assets to the world. Many of these people "walked in the supernatural" for a season but ended up embracing loose living and no longer even serve the Lord. They were totally unprepared for real-life situations where trial and testing simply do not go away with one prayer. If you are training and activating students into the prophetic and supernatural without preaching holiness and living righteously before the Lord, I ask you to repent and turn from this deception.

I have repented and will continue to repent of those years of walking in the deception that plagues so much of the "supernatural evangelism" that we witness today. If but one person wakes up to the reality that I am talking about and sees their own deception or helps another see theirs, it will be well worth it to me!

I will end this chapter with the words of one of my prophetic fathers, R. Loren Sandford, and pray that those who have read this will be awakened to the danger involved in prophetic and supernatural evangelism and allow God to bring refreshing to your heart as He did mine. Loren says, "If the goal is to be supernatural, you will end up in shipwreck. But if the goal is intimacy with Jesus, you will end up supernatural."

# CHAPTER 11

# PROPHETIC MINISTRY IN THE LOCAL
# CHURCH

O NE of my greatest concerns with parts of the contemporary prophetic movement is regarding how few prophets and prophetic
people actually attend a local church or any expression of one
in the body of Christ. I recently attended a large prophetic conference where one breakout session was titled, "Prophetic Ministry in
the Local Church." The room was packed and the speaker took the
stage. To my heartbreak, the prophet teaching the session did not even
attend a local church, and most of those in the audience did not either.
As I sat in the back, I thought to myself, "How can someone teach
'prophetic ministry in the local church' who doesn't attend a church
to people who don't either? How bizarre!"

As I have trained and interacted closely with prophets and prophetic people over the last ten years on a full-time basis, I have heard
numerous excuses and spiritualizations as to why prophets and prophetic people don't have to or need to attend a community of believers. Most of the reasons prophets and prophetic people have for why
they aren't accountable to anyone or aren't connected anywhere have

to do with being wounded and hurt by a church or church leader along their prophetic journey. Whether the hurt is valid or not, I believe it is against New Testament teaching and practice for prophets and prophetic people to be disconnected from some form of accountability and community.

I wrote in *I See a New Prophetic Generation*, "I see a radical restoration process being released to the body of Christ by the Father Himself between pastor/shepherds and the new prophetic generation. There will be levels of healing and repentance toward one another that have not been seen in any other generation. A key part of this restoration process is the decisive ending of a group of lone ranger prophets in the body of Christ who have no accountability and do not want to submit to any form of spiritual authority."

## DANGEROUS PROPHETS AND PROPHETIC PEOPLE

Dangerous prophets and prophetic people are those who refuse two main realities:

1. Community

2. Accountability.

A lifestyle of accountability and healthy community is required to operate at high levels consistently in the Spirit. Remember, non-accountable relationships mean that we develop a life in God without applying truth to ourselves. We can never be in control of our own accountability without being soft on our own immaturity and carnality.

I want to encourage and caution all those who follow prophets and prophetic people to make sure these messengers are actually involved in a real community of believers on a consistent basis and readily submit to some form of accountability. If they refuse community and oversight or even become angered by those seeking to find out if they have accountability in their life, they are a potential danger to the body of Christ. "I only answer to God," "I'm in the wilderness," and "I travel so much I have no time for community," should be immediate red flags for the body of Christ. We must reject the narrative that true prophets and prophetic people cannot function, mature, and be healthy within a local church.

## MATURING IN THE PROPHETIC

One of the strongholds that some prophets and prophetic people often deal with is that they are enamored with their gift, which they think makes them special, failing to realize that the gift must be developed and matured. In the words of John Paul Jackson, "If you are called to be a prophet, one of the first things you need to understand is that the calling makes you absolutely, positively nothing special. It actually makes you a potential failure—but it doesn't make you anything special, because 'many are called, but few are chosen' (Matthew 22:14). That statement is very true in the prophetic realm."

While the stories concerning many prophets and prophetic people controlling church leadership are valid and extremely painful at times, they do not speak for the entire prophetic movement. There is a serious spirit of rebellion and independence operating in much of the contemporary prophetic movement. Too many prophets and prophetic people want to minister in a local church that they aren't even a part of. They have no desire or intention to build community and relationship with anyone, yet they want to prophesy whenever they please. This is not prophetic maturity in action, but immaturity and foolishness.

Here are five ways that prophets and prophetic people can grow in maturity:

1. Seek constant feedback on the prophecies you give and cultivate a hunger for personal input from leaders. (Immature prophetic people view input from leaders as unbelief, disregarding the Lord, or raising your hand against the Lord's anointed.)

2. Develop a solid track record with regard to accuracy, humility, and teachability. (Immature prophetic people use their gifts for their own promotion and tend to be super-spiritual people who act like they have an exclusive relationship with God that somehow renders them outside of correction or challenge.)

3. Earn the privilege to prophesy in public meetings by your Christlikeness. (Immature prophetic people are prone to outbursts of anger, and often have little remorse for their actions. They have a victim mentality when challenged and justify their poor behavior rather than address it and be transformed.)

4. Be sensitive to any form of personal manipulation and control in the words you release. Test the spirit of your own prophecy. Apply the tests to your own word before you release it. (Immature prophetic people use their gifts for their own personal gain, including influence and financial increase. They always have an agenda. They need their filter purified.)

5.  The goal of your prophetic ministry in a body of believers is not to be seen as a threat or liability but as an asset and tremendous blessing from the hand of the Lord. (Immature prophetic people rarely build relationships of real worth and value. They minister on their own rather than in the godly confines of a team of people dedicated to a common purpose.)

# OPERATING IN A CORPORATE PROPHETIC ANOINTING

Being a prophet or prophetic person does not give us a right to walk into corporate church gatherings and use our gifting as a means to overthrow a meeting, even if the spirit behind the word given is well intentioned. Prophetic people are a part of the body of Christ. They have never been given a scriptural right to overtake public meetings in the name of being a messenger of God. If you believe God has a word for a corporate gathering, you need to take appropriate action and follow proper protocol. If you believe you have a word for the body, ask yourself these five questions:

1.  Is this a word God is speaking to me for the corporate body or for my own personal life?

2.  Do I sense that this word is for *this* service?

3.  If this word is for this service, in what manner should I give this word? (Delivery needs to match content.)

4.  Is my filter clear? (Do I have a judgmental or critical spirit against this church or its leadership?)

5.  Does the word seem to confirm or join the flow of the service?

If these questions have been asked and the word has passed the protocol, find a pastor or leader and submit the word to them. The key word is *submit* the word to them! We have to settle in our hearts as prophets and prophetic people that if the leadership does not feel that the word is for the congregation, then it is off of our conscience and it becomes an issue that they will have to take up with the Father. I cannot over-emphasize how much building relationship with pastors and leaders will help prophets and prophetic people with regard to prophetic ministry being readily welcomed in the Church.

# JUDGING AND TESTING PROPHECY

According to the Word of God, the body of Christ has a responsibility to judge and test prophetic words that are given. If prophets and prophetic people have an issue with their prophecies and lifestyles being held accountable, then they have an issue with God Himself. Prophetic ministry is not a game and is not a free-for-all. We must have authentic, purified, and accountable prophetic ministry restored to the Church. First Thessalonians 5:19-21 says, "Do not quench the Spirit; do not despise prophetic utterances. But examine everything carefully; hold fast to that which is good."

The body of Christ must not shut down prophetic ministry, but it also does not have to allow chaos and disorder in the name of "prophetic ministry." Remember, there are charismatics and then there is charismania! Believers in Jesus Christ are asked to examine prophecy carefully and hold on to the good. This requires seeking feedback and healthy dialogue concerning prophetic words that are ministered. Again, if prophets and prophetic people refuse community and accountability, they are rejecting the teachings of First Thessalonians 5:19-21 and Hebrews 10:25.

In First Corinthians 14:31-33 it says, "For you can all prophesy one by one, so that all may learn and all may be exhorted; and the spirits of prophets are subject to prophets; for God is not a God of confusion but of peace, as in all the churches of the saints."

Here again at Corinth, Paul is instructing them that prophetic ministry must be welcomed in the Church, but there must also be clear order and direction to it. How can prophets and prophetic people claim that they don't need community and accountability when Paul so clearly says that the spirits of prophets are subject to other prophets? It would actually appear and make more sense that prophets and prophetic people should be working closely together in the local church rather than floating around from city to city citing random Scriptures and past hurts to excuse their prophetic immaturity and rebellion.

If the contemporary prophetic movement is going to get cleansed and ignited, it must start with building healthy relationships with church leaders and saints. Having a prophetic gift, being called as a prophet, or even being hurt by the church in the past is not a valid and biblical excuse for why someone can't benefit or doesn't need to be a part of a local church. In the next chapter, I will highlight ten pitfalls and traps that speak directly to this issue of prophets and prophetic people needing to be connected and accountable to a local community of believers and leadership.

## PROPHETIC WORD REGARDING THE CHURCH

As I have continued to train, equip, and interact with thousands of prophets and prophetic people around the United States and the world, I have heard the consistent cry from them concerning the religious control, oppression, greed, etc. taking place in their region and city and how they just can't go to "church" anymore. While seeking the Lord regarding this cry, He began to give me a very clear vision and word for prophets and prophetic people regarding their issues and concerns with local churches and/or ministries, etc.

He revealed to me that there are three primary mandates He is releasing to prophets and prophetic people right now regarding the local church. They are as follows:

## 1. THE PLANTING OF NEW CHURCHES/MINISTRIES

It will not be enough in the days ahead for prophets and prophetic people to complain and cry out that every church in their area isn't allowing God to move, etc. God is beginning to birth a vision and dream down inside many prophets and prophetic people to give birth to prophetic communities and churches that will welcome the Holy Spirit and a love for the Word of God. Prophets and prophetic people must begin to be part of the solution and not limit themselves to pointing out the problem with much of the current wineskin of Church. Many prophets and prophetic people are going to be challenged to deal with their bitterness and hurt toward the Church and its leaders and actually become the change they so desire to see. There must be a realm of community and accountability formed within these new church plants and ministries. Whether it's a house church, mega church, or movie theatre church, the answer to the current problems in the Church is not for prophets and prophetic people to simply walk away and shut down their gifts. Bitterness will either shut down a prophetic person's gift or contaminate it. The prophets and prophetic people must find healing from their bitterness and unforgiveness toward the Church and its leaders and release a fresh and purified sound in the earth.

## 2. THE FAITHFULNESS TO THE ASSIGNMENT

Some prophets and prophetic people will and are receiving a mandate to be faithful to the assignment they have been given in a local church, even if that church is not fulfilling its destiny. God sends many prophets and prophetic people into local churches and ministries to be an asset and help to them. Many of these assignments require prophets and prophetic people to attend churches and ministries where they do not agree with everything and could even detect sin among the leadership or community. In these seasons, God is developing and maturing His prophets and prophetic people by allowing them to fellowship in His emotions and sorrow that His Spirit is being grieved and quenched. It is necessary in the life of every prophet and prophetic person to go through this experience. Many times you are sent into environments not to cry out in public but to learn how to intercede and travail in private. God is going to send many prophets and prophetic people into seeker-friendly churches without a public assignment but a mighty private one—prayer.

## 3. IT'S TIME TO MOVE GEOGRAPHICALLY

The third mandate God showed me He is releasing to prophets and prophetic people is actually calling them to move geographically to become a member of a community of believers where His Spirit is being poured out and the leadership is in alignment with the will of God. Many prophets and prophetic people are not currently living in the city that they are called to live in and will experience an intensified burden to move geographically. There are fathering prophets and apostles who are currently in church leadership that will begin to provide a safe haven for God's prophets and prophetic people and will be a mighty blessing.

Look for these three primary mandates to sweep the prophets and prophetic people in the days ahead. New prophetic churches and ministries are going to be planted, some prophets and prophetic people will be called to be faithful to the assignments God has given them in churches and ministries that they won't necessarily agree with, and others will be called to move geographically to sit under fathering prophets and apostles and learn how to develop deep relationships with the saints. The option to disconnect, quit, become a lone ranger, or become bitter and angry with the Church is not on the table. If the contemporary prophetic movement is to be cleansed and ignited, we must see a much greater commitment from prophets and prophetic people to become part of the family of God and the change we so desperately need in parts of the body of Christ.

# CHAPTER 12

# THE PITFALLS OF THE PROPHET'S
# MINISTRY

THE traps and pitfalls that are set along the path of true prophets are both serious and very dangerous. The devil knows how powerful pure and undefiled prophets are!

I believe God is raising up a company of prophets in the earth who will operate in purity, humility, and authenticity. We will now look at ten specific pitfalls or traps that will be discovered along the path of the prophet that will contaminate and pervert the gifting God has given them. If the prophets can avoid the following pitfalls and gain victory, incredible damage will be done to the devil's camp and a revival of purity and cleansing will sweep the contemporary prophetic movement.

## 1. THE PITFALL OF REFUSING WILDERNESS TRAINING

The training ground for all called prophets of God is the wilderness. This is the place where God draws His prophets to crucify and crush their ambitions, pride, arrogance, carnality, and anything that will get in the way of them becoming pure vessels for His Spirit to move through. It is in the wilderness where the personal desires of prophets die and the desires of God come alive. Craving platforms, microphones, and a travel itinerary is crucified and crushed in the wilderness.

Biblically speaking, there is a calling, consecration, and then a commissioning. Too many believe that because God has called them, they have now been commissioned into prophetic ministry. This is not the truth and forsakes the most important and crucial development of the prophet—consecration. The consecration process, which will be repeated numerous times throughout the life of a prophet, is known as the wilderness.

One of the greatest pitfalls of prophetic ministry is when prophets refuse wilderness training. When prophets are not trained in hiddenness, they crave the platform and know nothing of the prayer room. They will chase after the applause of men because they have never heard the Father affirming them in secret. When prophets refuse wilderness training, they will desire fame and fortune over holiness and repentance. Prophets who refuse wilderness training will tear down with their character what their prophetic gifting has built. The wilderness is where God creates a place inside of the prophets for them to carry His heart with pure and undefiled intentions and motives. Prophets who have not been wilderness trained make prophetic ministry all about them, their influence, and their success. Prophets who have been wilderness trained do not fear men; they live for the glory of God and value the secret place over any public space.

## 2. THE PITFALL OF PROFILING OTHERS

In First Samuel 16, we find Samuel the prophet going to anoint the second king of Israel. On his search for the next king, God gives

Samuel incredible prophetic instruction in verse 7 as He says, "But the Lord said to Samuel, 'Do not look at his appearance or at the height of his stature, because I have rejected him; for God sees not as man sees, for man looks at the outward appearance, but the Lord looks at the heart.'"

One of the most common mistakes that prophets can make is giving someone a prophetic word based upon their outward appearance, stature, or behavior. I call this "prophetic profiling." Samuel noticed Eliab because of his outward appearance and said, "Surely the Lord's anointed is before Him," but this was not the case. As prophets of God, we must be very careful that we do not become consumed or distracted by looking for outward clues or appearances to help us form the prophecies that we give.

For example, several years ago I ministered at a conference where two men in the front row were dressed completely opposite of one another. One man was wearing a three-piece suit with fine jewelry. The other man was wearing blue jeans, a plain white t-shirt, and dirty looking shoes. God had given me a prophetic word about a season of financial increase coming and specific business deals regarding the oil industry that were being released. As I looked at these two men in the natural, it would have been very easy to stand up the man in the three-piece suit because of his stature or appearance. As I prayed, God showed me that the prophetic word was for the man in the blue jeans, t-shirt, and the tattered shoes. As I released the prophetic word, he was powerfully touched by the Spirit. After the meeting, he came up to me and said he was a multi-million dollar businessman who worked in the oil industry, but rarely wore nice clothing.

We must be very cautious not to profile people based on their outward appearance, race, gender, etc. and hear from the Lord regardless of what they look like on the outside.

# 3. THE PITFALL OF SANCTIFIED PSYCHIC READING

In First Kings 22, the prophet Micaiah stood before king Ahab and king Jehoshaphat and was asked to give them the word of the Lord. Prior to this, the kings had already consulted and received prophetic ministry from the other 400 prophets in the land. The prophets had told Ahab and Jehoshaphat to, "Go up, for the Lord will give it [Ramoth-gilead] into the hand of the king." When pressed, Micaiah told the kings that God would not give them victory and that Ahab would die. What was the primary difference between the 400 prophets and the lone prophet Micaiah?

The 400 prophets read the hearts of the kings back to them, but Micaiah read the heart of God back to the kings. We must be very careful as we prophesy to people that we are not reading their own hearts' desires back to them. Prophets are feelers and burden bearers. It is very easy to pick up on the emotions, feelings, and even desires that are resting inside the hearts of people. What happens if what people are feeling or desiring to do is not from God? What if they have selfish ambitions, greed, and lust in their hearts and we simply go up and confirm what's not of God inside of them?

For example, I once ministered with a prophet in Indiana who called a family out of a crowd with several words of knowledge he believed he had. He said he heard, "California," "millions of dollars," and "large house and nice cars." As he spoke this over the family, they fell down weeping and then got up and rejoiced. At the end of the meeting, they wrote him a ten thousand dollar check and he thanked them. From there, the family moved from Indiana to California with the supposed "word of the Lord." They were supposed to move to California where they were going to make millions of dollars and live in a large house and have nice cars. As the story goes, they lasted two years in California with no open doors, no money coming in, and no nice house or cars. What happened?

I would like to suggest that the prophet simply read their own hearts back to them and never discerned what the heart of God was for them. As prophets, we are learning how to distinguish what's in the heart of man versus what is in the heart of God. Witches and psychics can prophesy what's in the heart of man, but only prophets of God can prophesy what's in the heart of God because they have access to it. Prophets must not get involved in sanctified psychic reading.

# 4. THE PITFALL OF MAMMON

The spirit of witchcraft (manipulation and control) will seek to overtake the prophets of God by using money, promotion, and material possessions to contaminate and pollute what God is actually saying.

I see a trend rising in the Church in which prophets are acting like and even being treated as magicians, prostitutes, and pimps. On stages and throughout the Internet, many offer their prophetic services to anyone who can fill their pockets with money, promote their ministry, and fuel book sales. These men and women are acting like modern-day prophetic whores. They find stimulation through stroking the ego and flesh of leaders and people, all at the expense of the purity and fresh anointing that we so desperately need in the prophetic movement.

Like Hophni and Phinehas (see 1 Sam. 2), these con artists are engaging in wickedness and sin in the house of God because they treat that which is holy and pure as casual and oftentimes as a joke. The spirit of mammon has devoured these "prophets for hire." They have been ravaged by a greed for financial gain and a lust to be treated with all the perks and accommodations that a Hollywood actor would be given.

Just as Jeremiah declared in Jeremiah 23:13, many prophets in America are "prophesying by Baal" and leading the body of Christ astray. The Baal spirit has caused the prophets' focus and concern to be health, wealth, and prosperity, when they should be agonizing over the sin of the nation and travailing over how to bring forth messages of repentance, reformation, and revival. The goal has become to stroke the people to sleep, when God desires to provoke His people to change in this hour.

Some very well-known contemporary prophets now even require people to scan their credit card or sow a large seed offering if they want to receive a word from God. It is extremely grieving to the Holy Spirit that people will actually line up by the droves to pay these prophetic prostitutes for these illicit spiritual "favors."

It is impossible for prophets to minister in this kind of atmosphere without partnering with the spirit of witchcraft. Many church leaders who have themselves lost the fresh anointing of the Holy Spirit and are now leading failing ministries are inviting prophetic voices into their ministries in an attempt to gather large offerings and bolster their declining attendance. They are Sauls looking for Samuels to prop them up. These prophets and leaders have made a demonic covenant with mammon and witchcraft before the prophetic meetings ever begin. This sick and twisted practice not only scams the people of God, but God is nowhere to be found in the midst of this evil idolatry!

# 5. THE PITFALL OF THE LONE RANGER

In the Old Testament, the prophets were the singular voice of God to the nation. They came and went as they pleased and prophesied to the kings and the nation. In the New Testament, Jesus Christ has become the mediator between God and man (see 1 Tim 2:5) and now has given all believers the Holy Spirit to lead and guide them into the truth. The role of New Testament prophets is not the same as Old Testament prophets. New Testament prophets have now become a part of the body of Christ. They no longer prophesy as "outsiders" but as those who are in love with the body of Christ and actively serving and accountable to her. Prophets are not islands of revelation unto themselves. They need accountability and community.

I want to encourage all prophets to make sure you are actually involved in a real community of believers on a consistent basis and readily submit to some form of accountability. If prophets refuse community and oversight or even become angered by those seeking to find out if they have accountability, they are a potential danger to the body of Christ. "I only answer to God" or "I travel so much I have no time for community" should be an immediate red flag.

# 6. THE PITFALL OF PRIDE

Prophets must remember that they only see in part (see 1 Cor. 13:9). Pride is a swollen estimation of one's own importance. Prophets must be careful that they don't become prideful when people praise them for giving an accurate prophetic word or thinking they have more authority than they actually do. The truth is that prophets need the other four ministries of apostles, teachers, pastors, and evangelists (see Eph. 4:11) to help mature and grow their own gifting and calling. I will speak more to this issue in the next chapter.

# 7. THE PITFALL OF ADRENALINE AND EMOTIONALISM

As prophets of God, we are called to minister from the place of peace, not pressure. We will constantly be placed in environments full of hype, loud music, and the carnal desires of people. The prophet Jeremiah commented on the prophetic movement and leaders in his day and said, "An appalling and horrible thing has happened in the land: the prophets prophesy falsely, and the priests rule on their own authority; and *My people love it so!*" (Jer. 5:30-31, emphasis mine). Jeremiah lived in a day when people actually loved false prophecy. They loved being told what they wanted to hear and not what they needed to hear.

If people are addicted to adrenaline, they will be drawn to what gets their blood pumping and their heart pounding. They will only listen to what gets them stirred up and will gravitate toward prophetic voices who will do that for them. In this process, they will blind themselves to whether these prophetic voices even have a history of accuracy. They will forget to examine whether their prophetic words passed the test of Scriptures and truly advanced the kingdom of God.

Our polluted prophetic stream too often delivers what we are prepared to hear or what we think about ourselves. If you have problems with covenant relationships and commitment, you will hear God telling you to move from church to church.

If you carry a root of insecurity and have contracted an infection of ambition or arrogance to cover it, you will hear "from God" all kinds of exalted things about yourself. You will gravitate toward prophetic voices that will flatter that delusory image. You will hear these things and draw them out of people you regard as prophetic voices.

# 8. THE PITFALL OF GIVING HOROSCOPE PROPHECY

There is a modern-day phenomenon taking place within the contemporary prophetic movement that I believe must be confronted and specifically addressed with love and truth. The sensation I speak of regards the increase and explosion of very general and vague prophetic words being posted on social media and released on popular Christian websites that have little to no *substance* or *specifics*. And because of the lack of content and specifics within the prophetic words, there is no place for *accountability* or even judging the *accuracy* of what is supposedly being said by God. Let me give you some examples of vague and general prophecy that lacks substance, specifics, and even accountability.

For starters, these prophecies are directed at *anyone and everyone*. There is no target audience, person, or group of people whom the prophetic word is specifically directed to. In other words, it's a horoscope prophecy. How it works is that people simply scan the Facebook posts of popular prophetic voices trying to find a status or prophetic video that they can apply to their life or they scan popular Christian websites looking for the latest prophetic word released that again is typically not addressed to a target audience, person, or groups of people and has absolutely no substance or specifics. It's a bunch of fluff that has someone's carnal desires and greed at its core. This is horoscope prophecy.

Second, these prophecies do not ask for participation, sacrifice, or requirements for those the word is supposedly for. It's pretty much a name it and claim it one-stop showboat. All someone has to do is read the word on social media, claim their prize, and *bada bing bada boom*, your destiny and desires *will be* fulfilled.

The explosion and increase of general and vague prophecy across the Internet world can be likened to going to a Chinese restaurant and getting a free fortune cookie. Pick one, open it up, and there you have your horoscope prophecy.

The heartbreaking part about all of this is that when we turn to the Scriptures to try and find where all this vague and general prophecy is coming from, *you can't find any.* You cannot find a single prophet or prophetic word in Scripture that was not prophesying to a specific person, people group, or nation and what they prophesied was not only *specific* and full of *substance*, but it also had *requirements* from those who received it.

There is so much more to the prophetic movement than promising anyone and everyone upgrades, breakthrough, financial blessing, more glory, angel feathers, gold dust, property, and more. People can keep scrolling Facebook and popular Christian websites for their monthly prophetic horoscope, but I believe that God is calling many of His people to hit "delete" and unsubscribe from all these shenanigans and tomfoolery.

God is raising up a company of prophetic messengers, intercessors, and saints who are hungry for a word of the Lord that has weight, substance, and specifics. They are hungry for revelatory prophecy, not spontaneous prophecy. They must not be ashamed of their appetite for the deeper and weightier matters that are upon God's heart.

May we heed the warning that Jeremiah gave in his day when God said, "I did not send these prophets, but they ran. I did not speak to them, but they prophesied" (Jer. 23:21).

# 9. THE PITFALL OF BECOMING A VENDING MACHINE

Prophetic maturity is not measured by whether we have a prophetic word for every world event or situation, but rather whether we know when to remain silent when we do not have a word from the Lord. I want to encourage prophets not to succumb to the pressure of feeling like you have to put out a "new prophetic word" every day, week, or month. The contemporary prophetic movement has worshiped the giving of personal prophecy to such a degree that now prophets have forsaken their primary calling—to turn the people back to the living God, not read their mail all day.

You are not a vending machine. You should not be expected or even feel the need to pop out prophetic words every time someone sows a "seed" into you or stops to look at the "goods" you have inside. I'm convinced that much of what fuels the pressure to put out a prophetic word every day, week, or month is the need to keep fans and followers happy, to get people to keep giving financially, and worst of all to feed a deep inner need inside the prophet for validation through popularity and fortune.

I fear that many prophets on social media have built a following of people who are always itching to hear something new, something sensational, something entertaining, and something pleasing to their flesh. These deceived Christians are like the Athenians in Acts 17:21

who spent their time on nothing else than either telling or listening for some new thing.

Prophets! Do not fall for this trap! Stop popping out "new prophetic words" just so you can get more "likes" and "followers" on social media. Stop popping out "new prophetic words" that have no substance or specifics and literally could be applied to anything and everything. Has God really spoken to you or has He not? You must recognize that there are prophets prophesying whom God has not spoken to and prophets traveling and ministering whom God has not sent (see Jer. 23).

I'm praying that God would deliver a generation of prophets from the need to pop out new prophetic words so they can be validated by men, and He will raise up a generation of prophets who will only speak when God speaks, even if it's just once a year and unpopular.

Prophets! Fight the pressure. Do not give in to carnality and popularity contests. Do not allow the people of God to treat you like a vending machine and do not act like one regardless. Have the courage to remain silent when God has not spoken to you and commit to never compromising the word of the Lord no matter what open doors come your way.

# 10. THE PITFALL OF CARRYING REJECTION

To be called as a prophet of the Lord is to share and partake in the sufferings of Christ. One of those sufferings and cups to drink that cannot be passed on is certainly the cup of rejection (see Isa. 53:3). Rejection is extremely painful, especially when it comes from family members, friends, and people in ministry you thought you could trust. I imagine the pain of what Jesus must have experienced in the

Garden of Gethsemane or perhaps even at Calvary, being rejected and despised even by those closest to Him.

It only takes a cursory reading of all the Old Testament prophets to understand that they too were men who were deeply rejected. What about the New Testament? John the Baptist was rejected, Jesus Christ was rejected, and many of the prophets who came after Him continued to be rejected. In fact, Scripture is clear that one of the signs of a false prophet is that everyone loves everything they prophesy (Jer. 5:31). In the words of Jesus, He said, "Woe to you when all men speak well of you" (Luke 6:26).

According to the testimony of both the prophets themselves and Jesus Christ, there is no way around rejection if you are truly called as a prophet of the Lord. You must receive rejection as part of your prophetic training, but choose not to operate in a spirit of rejection. This is where the path of a prophet and the need for healthy and mature development can become very difficult. As a prophet of the Lord, you will be trained by the rejection of men, but it is not healthy, nor is it the will of God, that you walk in a spirit of rejection. When prophets operate out of a spirit of rejection, they are convinced that they are constantly "alone" in their calling and everyone is either against them now or will be in the future.

The spirit of rejection operating in a wounded prophet's life has convinced them that it's them versus the world and they are out to prove everyone wrong. The motive of the heart behind prophets who operate out of the spirit of rejection is to show the world and religion how bad they missed it with them. These prophets with wounds of rejection have what I call a "told you so" approach to life and ministry. Every open door and potential favor that God gives them, in their eyes, is twisted into proving to their critics how anointed they really were in the first place. These types of attitudes and heart postures are not only signs that a prophet is operating in a spirit of rejection, but they are extremely grieving to God the Father and not a sign of a mature prophetic anointing.

# CHAPTER 13

# PROPHETS AND THE FIVE-FOLD
# MINISTRY

I N Ephesians 4:11-13, Paul lists five ministries (apostles, prophets, teachers, pastors, evangelists) that God has given some in the body of Christ for the equipping of the saints until we reach the unity of the faith and the knowledge of the Son of God. I want to be faithful to point out that Paul said God gave "some" to fill these offices.

As referenced in Chapter 4, one of the major issues plaguing the body of Christ is delusions of grandeur. We live in a church culture where everyone believes they have a call to be a five-fold minister, when Scripture speaks to the contrary. Until we have unity in the body of Christ and the full knowledge of the Son of God, these five ministries must operate and be embraced in our midst. For example, if "pastors" and "teachers" are the only two ministries allowed to operate in the church, we are receiving only two fifths of the ministry that Christ intended us to partake of.

Some arrogant church leaders have stated that they themselves have all five ministries. In other words, they believe they are an apostle, prophet, teacher, pastor, and evangelist. In the example of Paul, he referred to himself as an apostle, teacher, and preacher (see 2 Tim. 1:11) but nowhere in Scripture does Paul say he was a prophet or evangelist. At best, I believe those who have a five-fold ministry calling have a primary office they operate in with a secondary one, but it is simply not true that one individual can operate in all five ministries. They can be an apostle and be prophetic but that does not make them an apostle as well as a prophet, etc.

Concerning prophets, it's vitally important that we recognize that we must work with the other four ministries God has given the Church in order for there to be full unity and the knowledge of the Son of God. Prophets were constantly working with other five-fold ministers in the New Testament. There were prophets and teachers at Antioch. Paul, an apostle, traveled with Silas who was a prophet, and so on. I believe the prophetic purity and cleansing we need today will come as prophets recognize and confess their need for apostles, teachers, pastors, and evangelists to reach unity and a complete revelation of who Jesus Christ really is.

## PROPHETS NEED APOSTLES

Prophets have the tendency to wander around in circles because their eyes are so focused on the future. They desperately need apostles to help them to build and live for the present. Prophets constantly get caught chasing never-ending revelation and pursuing new spiritual experiences. They need apostles to hold their feet to the fire to study and actually know the Word of God. Prophets are prone to wander around and become lone rangers. They need apostles to father them, work alongside them, instruct them, and correct them.

Apostles help the prophets find their orientation and direction. Apostles will establish kingdom government in the lives of prophets and bring great emotional balance and stability to them. In many ways, apostles act as the anchor to the prophet's ministry (see Eph. 2:20).

Apostles and prophets must learn how to function together as a team in this hour. Every apostle needs a prophet and every prophet needs an apostle (see 1 Cor. 12:28). The prophets bring great confirmation and revelation to God's apostles and the apostles bring great emotional stability and balance to the prophets of God. Healthy prophets are always connected to fathering apostles and healthy apostles are always connected to revelatory prophets. We must learn how to work together and not compete against one another in the days we are living in.

## PROPHETS NEED TEACHERS

There is a reason why in First Corinthians 12:28 prophets are specifically placed in between apostles and teachers when it comes to establishing the kingdom of God and the New Testament Church. When prophets do not have apostles *and* teachers as their boundary lines, they go off into dangerous doctrine and immature behavior.

Prophets have the tendency to form their own doctrine based off of their spiritual experiences. Teachers will call the prophets into line and ask them, "Where is that found in the Scriptures?" Rebellious prophets who answer to no one constantly mislabel God's teachers as religious and constricting when really they are operating in their divine purpose and function. Teachers help many prophets to realize that their good-sounding "revelation" actually can't be backed up in the Word of God and needs to be thrown out. Just because it sounds good to preach does not at all mean it's biblical. Healthy and mature prophets constantly submit their dreams, visions, and revelations to teachers before they ever release what they believe God has spoken or shown to them. Teachers are the checks and balances that prophets so desperately need.

Teachers function in a line-upon-line, precept-upon-precept reality when it comes to the kingdom of God, whereas prophets tend to function in a dream-after-dream, vision-after-vision, spiritual experience after spiritual experience reality. While prophets and teachers each have their own function, they desperately need one another to bring balance to one another's ministries.

Teachers help prophets to unpack and thoroughly investigate the dreams, visions, and revelations they receive. They challenge prophets to seek God for more insight and clarity regarding what they are seeing and hearing. Without teachers, prophets are potential candidates for heretical doctrine based off of bizarre experience alone. They risk not being rooted and grounded in the Word of God by teachers, and most importantly they will not grow in character and integrity without teachers taking them to task over whether their lifestyles line up with who God is and what He has revealed in His Word.

Prophets, you must surround yourself with apostles and teachers. You are not an island of revelation unto yourself! You are not the only one who "hears" and "sees" God. Let's grow in maturity and confess our great need of one another.

## PROPHETS NEED PASTORS

Without the influence of pastors, prophets have the tendency to be harsh, arrogant, and disconnected from the saints. These two five-fold ministries are the hardest to get to work together, but are also the most effective when they get along.

Pastors impart compassion, tenderness, and personal care for the prophets. Without strong pastoral care, prophets remain wounded in their souls due to the amount of rejection that they face because of their calling. Pastors are focused on the present issues at hand while prophets are caught up in the future. Pastors typically slow things down while prophets want to speed things up.

Pastors desire to counsel people while prophets would prefer to just cast the demons out. Pastors will sit with hurting and broken people for hours while the prophets want a quick solution now. Prophets just want to prophesy and leave, but pastors are willing to walk through the pain and trials of those who receive the prophetic ministry. Pastors love hospital visitation and more, while prophets just want to walk in and raise the dead real quick.

Every prophet needs a pastor and every pastor needs a prophet. Prophets like to focus on maturing saints at an accelerated pace while pastors take time for the hurting, broken, and wounded. Pastors stroke, but prophets provoke. Pastors coddle, but prophets cut. Pastors comfort, but prophets correct. Pastors stimulate, but prophets impregnate. Pastors listen, but prophets challenge.

When prophets choose to join themselves with a pastor, they are greatly balanced and matured!

Both of these ministries are so important and though they have separate functions, they must learn how to work together. Prophets are never given permission to be lone rangers, and pastors have the difficult function of teaching prophets the joy of living in community and learning how to grow in love toward God's people. The most unstable and immature prophets I have worked with around the globe are always those who refuse pastoral care for their own lives and don't think they need community with one family of believers.

## PROPHETS NEED EVANGELISTS

Evangelists stir up a vision for the harvest in the lives of prophets. They challenge them to prophesy beyond the four walls of a church and into the harvest fields. Without the influence of evangelists, prophets will be nearsighted in their approach to the kingdom of God and will constantly focus on prophesying to those who already know God. They will forget the lost who must be prophesied into the kingdom of God.

Evangelists thrust prophets into the harvest fields. At times prophets can tend to be harsh and intense with what God is saying. Evangelists help prophets to impart a revelation of the mercy and grace of God toward sinners. Evangelists teach prophets how to grow beyond using "churchy" terminology when they prophesy to the lost and help them get to the heart of the matter. Evangelists teach prophets that the word of the Lord can run swiftly at the gas station or in the grocery store.

## THE DAYS AHEAD

In the days ahead we are going to witness a mature company of apostles, prophets, teachers, pastors, and evangelists who will work and walk together and get over their pride, insecurity, and jealousy. God is raising up prophets who will connect with other five-fold ministers and they will carry a unique perspective and grace in the days ahead.

# CHAPTER 14

# A VISION OF THE COMING

# DAYS

A prophetic reformation is underway that will change the landscape of the contemporary prophetic movement forever. The vision of the coming days is both exciting and sobering. There will be three primary subject matters that will highlight this move of God in the contemporary prophetic movement. They will be:

1. Repentance

2. Fathering

3. The Return of the Lord

## 1. REPENTANCE

The primary calling of a mature prophet is not to give personal prophecy but to turn and/or direct the people back to God by establishing a clear plumb line in Scripture. There is a standard of righteousness that must be established in any nation for true revival and awakening to come and God oftentimes uses His prophets to highlight and make clear that standard. Loren Sandford correctly wrote and said:

> Every past revival in Christian history has been based on a foundational cultural agreement concerning right and wrong, sin and morality. When society departed from that foundation, everyone knew it. As a result, people could respond to great preaching, feel guilt over their sin, turn to God and repent. Revival grew and spread on the basis of repentance and the forgiveness that flows from the cross and the blood, in large part because everyone understood the baseline from which they had departed and to which they could return. No such cultural agreement now exists. ...Without a sense of sin, repentance cannot come, and without repentance revival in the fullest sense cannot happen.[1]

Just as John the Baptist cried out with a message of repentance prior to the first coming of the Lord, so there will be another generation of end-time messengers who will cry out with a message of repentance prior to the second coming of the Lord. These burning and shining lamps will carry an anointing to break up the fallow ground of the hearts around them.

## REPENTANCE PREPARES THE WAY FOR REVIVAL

It was Frank Bartleman from the Asuza Street revival who said, "The depth of any revival will be determined exactly by the spirit of repentance that is obtained. In fact, this is the key to every true revival born of God."[2] If we want God to bring a Third Great Awakening, then we must prepare the way by preaching repentance to all men! How many churches, ministries, and leaders are crying out for revival yet are not preaching repentance? We need to get back to reading the Word of God!

John the Baptist's *message* was simple: "Repent, for the kingdom of heaven is near." John the Baptist's *baptism* was blunt: "I baptize with water for repentance." John the Baptist's *lifestyle* was challenging: "Produce fruit in keeping with repentance." It is this message, baptism, and lifestyle of repentance that will prepare the way for the next move of God.

## THE MESSENGER OF SATAN

Several years ago, I had a powerful prophetic dream that specifically revealed this vision of the coming days as it pertains to the need for repentance in the Church. In the dream, I saw a gigantic messenger of Satan coming into the United States from the East Coast. I called out to it from the walls of a large fortified city and said, "I am a watchman over this land and I command you to tell me, by what authority do you enter this nation?" It said, "I come here by the permission of the Church who has granted me access to come plunder and devour right in the midst of them."

The principality had the wings of an angel but the tail of a dragon, and it looked hideous! There was great darkness upon it, yet it had the outward appearance of unusual light. In its hands it carried a large black book with the words written on it: "The gospel of accommodation."

The Spirit began to show me massive deception is sweeping the Church and it is fast asleep. There is a very real war in the spirit realm over the true gospel, the gospel of self-denial, and this false gospel, the gospel of accommodation that is seeking to overtake the Church. The gospel of accommodation encourages Christians to fit Jesus into their life, rather than making Him their life. This false gospel requires no sacrifice, no commitment, and no death to self. It is dangerous, deceptive, and we are going to witness God beginning to highlight preachers and churches who preach this false gospel of accommodation. Prophetic messengers of repentance will emerge to confront this heresy.

## THE PAUL REVERE ANOINTING

As the Spirit spoke this to me in the dream, there was an army of horse riders waiting and prepared to run. I relayed to them what I had seen and I shouted, "The anointing of Paul Revere is upon us! Now is the time to warn the Church of the coming spiritual storms. We must warn them of the false gospel of accommodation!" If they give in, they will look no different from the world. Days are coming when a harlot Church will marry itself to the world, but an army will rise that will marry itself to the coming King of War. As I and the army of horse riders rode with the anointing of Paul Revere to churches, we visited three specific types of churches.

## THE SLEEPING CHURCH

The first type of church we visited had "Sleeping Church" engraved on its doors. As we opened the doors to these churches, every one of them was in the middle of a service. We would hurry in to relay the message of what we had just seen and heard, only to be shocked to see everyone in attendance, including the leadership, sucking on pacifiers. While this type of church could hear our words, they had no ability to respond. We began to cry out and say, "Why are you silent, Church, why are you silent? Though you are awake, you are sleeping!"

In the dream, the Holy Spirit immediately spoke to me Ephesians 4:14: "Then we will no longer be infants, tossed back and forth by the waves, and blown here and there by every wind of teaching and by the cunning and craftiness of people in their deceitful scheming" (NIV).

## THE HYPER-GRACE CHURCH

The second type of church we visited met in various looking buildings and was very postmodern. We were delighted because many of them seemed to be younger in age (18 to 35). As we warned them of the coming spiritual storms, they laughed at us. God said, "These are the products of the works-based gospel movement of the '80s and '90s. These are they who have rebelled in the name of grace, but not in the name of My Son." As the Spirit spoke this to us, there began to be mass commotion among them. He said, "These types of churches are blinding the generations to the truth in the name of grace. They call themselves Joel's army because they believe they will usher in the last-days grace movement in the earth, but know that they are like the locust seeking to devour and ravage the vineyards of young generations. They distort the truth and preach rebellion and tolerance in the name of grace. They shall question if hell exists. They will believe that many paths lead to Me."

After visiting these two types of churches, the horse riders were in great distress. I cried out to the Spirit and said, "Take me to Your church." I immediately rode up on a church building that had "Surrendered Church" on its doors.

## THE SURRENDERED CHURCH

We quickly walked in and sat down. I immediately noticed that in the back of this church was a gaping hole. It was as if a blast had gone off and almost entirely knocked out the back walls of the Surrendered Church. As we visited surrendered churches, we found the exact same thing. I sat in the back and asked the Father what had happened. He said, "My church was at first deceived by the false gospel of accommodation. The Hyper-Grace Church you just saw stormed out of the back of My church and left because of the preaching of holiness and the fear of the Lord, but now My Church has been awakened and it shall be repaired."

I got up out of my seat and watched as many people were working on repairing the gaping hole in the back of the church. As I watched, I noticed something interesting—the workers were not just any workers. They were true apostles and prophets restoring the foundation of the Church and many of them were teaching other young people how to properly lay the foundation. God said, "I am raising up a remnant in the Church that will be sound in doctrine and they will embrace the gospel of self-denial.

Many intercessors were in great travail, repenting over the sins of the Church, but having a great sense of hope as they cried out and thanked the Father for awakening the Church from deception. Then I woke up.

# 2. FATHERING

The prophetic reformation coming to the contemporary prophetic movement will involve a realm of fathering like we have never seen before. The cleansing and igniting that must take place cannot happen without proper community and accountability. As the Church begins to understand and embrace the difference between believers who operate in the gift of prophecy and those who operate in the office of prophet, fathering will help keep the prophets delivering the word of the Lord with the heart of the Lord. The fathering the prophets will undergo will help to humble them and keep them pure. Without proper fathering, it will take many prophets more than 20 years to fully mature and develop their gift. Some will never mature because they refuse relationship and correction.

## FATHERS, SONS, AND THE BEAUTIFUL MAN

I had a powerful prophetic dream recently where I saw hundreds of one-on-one gatherings with fathers and sons. Most of the sons were in their 20s and 30s, and the fathers were in their 50s and 60s. The gatherings were all the same. The fathers began to ask the sons how they were doing. Immediately, the sons began to list all their accomplishments and all the success they recently had. The fathers immediately rebuked the sons for their pride and arrogance. Every single meeting resulted in a shouting match. In the dream, I was overcome by deep grief watching all of this. Intense heartache and pain gripped me to my core.

What happened next caused me to intensely weep in the dream. A man glowing with bright light, a long white robe, and a golden sash around his shoulder appeared on the scene. His hair, facial features, and eyes were stunningly beautiful.

He walked up and began to place his hand on each of the fathers' shoulders and say, "Are you listening to the cry of your son? This is not pride and arrogance that you are hearing but a deep need to be validated and affirmed by you." Suddenly the beautiful man pulled a large bottle of liquid honey out of his white robe and poured it on the heads of the fathers. Tears began to stream down their faces and they wept.

The beautiful man held each of the fathers in his arms and said, "Even as My Father has loved, validated, and affirmed me as His Son, so I give to you this same grace now to love, validate, and affirm your sons. What your earthly fathers could not do for you, I am now releasing in the earth, for the fathers and sons must walk together in greater measures than ever before. I am calling on the fathers to look beyond the arrogance and pride to the real cry of the sons in this generation. You must not throw them away. I am going to mantle this generation of fathers with astounding patience, long-suffering, and mercy. Their fatherly maturity with swallow up the immaturity of the sons. For this is my kind intention of My will being manifested in the earth for such a time as this."

I immediately woke up from the dream with tears staining my pillow. Suddenly out of my heart erupted: "Thank You, Father! For You will fulfill Your words from Malachi 4:5-6 in these marvelous days that we now living in!"

> *Behold, I am going to send you Elijah the prophet before the coming of the great and terrible day of the Lord. He will restore the hearts of the fathers to their children and the hearts of the children to their fathers, so that I will not come and smite the land with a curse.*

Hope, healing, and reconciliation will mark the contemporary prophetic movement in these last days as companies of prophets learn how to navigate generationally with forgiveness and understanding toward one another. We must reject lone ranger prophetic ministry. Iron sharpens iron, and while the message of repentance will go forth, fathering will help to make sure the word of the Lord is being delivered with the heart of the Lord.

## 3. THE RETURN OF THE LORD

Second Peter 3:3-4 says, "Know this first of all, that in the last days mockers will come with their mocking, following after their own lusts, and saying, 'Where is the promise of His coming?'" The final area God showed me He would highlight in the contemporary prophetic movement is regarding the return of Jesus Christ. God recently said to me, "Beware of a scoffing spirit that is spreading like cancer in My body concerning the return of My Son, Jesus. There will be false teachers, prophets, and apostles who will rise in the earth who will scoff at these last days and claim that My Son has already returned and will not come again. They will not teach on the reality of hell, the fear of My name, nor the urgency of the hour that you live in. They are killing the zeal and passion that I'm desiring to arouse in My Bride prior to the sending of My Bridegroom Son. You must look for those who accurately handle My word of truth."

He continued, "In order to eradicate the cancer from the body, I am raising up end-time prophetic messengers who will cry aloud and spare not. They will challenge and confront these false apostles, prophets, and teachers like never before. As the Scriptures say, the faith of many will be upset over this growing cancer in My body. The cancer is not only limited to the teaching that My Son has already come or will not return, but also the scoffing spirit that will reject the call for urgency and holiness in the body. You are about to witness the high-lighting, focus, and emphasis of the return of My Son in the earth like never before. I'm going to mark and grip messengers with My holy fire that will leave them blessed with groaning and travail. You will see two contending movements that will rise in the body in the days ahead," says God. "One movement will seek to pacify and put the body to sleep as the cancer spreads, and another opposing movement will cry out for the return of My Son Jesus and warn the body of their need to be sober and alert in these days that you live in," says the Lord.

## DAY-OF-THE-LORD MESSENGERS

As the return of Jesus Christ draws near, we will witness the rise of "day of the Lord" prophetic messengers in our midst. I hear God saying, "I am currently anointing 'Day-of-the-Lord messengers' who will inspire and alarm My people and cause their hearts to be strong in faith with trembling. These burning ones will have a shock and awe effect wherever they minister. Some in the audience will run out the doors while many run down to the altars under deep conviction and travail. These prophetic messengers will be labeled radical and critical by the lukewarm."

These forerunners will proclaim both the great and terrible aspects of the Day of the Lord. Day-of-the-Lord preachers and prophets have never been popular, but they have been used to change history. Thank God for men the likes of Jonathan Edwards, Leonard Ravenhill, David Wilkerson, and A.W. Tozer. These day-of-the-Lord type messengers will specifically preach and prophesy concerning:

1.  Jesus: the King and Judge

2.  The fear of the Lord

3.  The wrath of God

4.  Eternal damnation

5.  The total depravity of man

6.  The urgency of the hour

7.  The gift of repentance and holiness

8.  Solemn assemblies and fasting

9.  The oil of intimacy

10. The throne-room reality

The greatest blessing the Day-of-the-Lord messengers will bring to the body of Christ is they will prepare us for the days ahead! They will operate with great power and authority, but they will also call for repentance and a turning to the Lord.

# I WENT TO HELL AND WAS STUNNED

Several months ago while I was extensively studying Matthew 7:22-24 and asking God for increased revelation, I had one of the most disturbing prophetic dreams of my life. The Scripture I was studying in Matthew says, "Many will say to Me on that day, 'Lord, Lord, did we not prophesy in Your name, and in Your name cast out demons, and in Your name perform many miracles?' And then I will declare to them, 'I never knew you; depart from Me, you who practice lawlessness.'"

In the prophetic dream, I was taken to hell where I saw all these ministers and individuals who had performed miracles, cast out demons, and prophesied. What I was shown next, I will never forget.

The Holy Spirit showed me long lines of people behind all of these ministers and individuals. He immediately revealed to me that these were all the people who had received the miracles, prophecies, and had been at one time delivered. As I gazed at the people in these lines, He said to me, "Did they not *receive* miracles, prophecy, and deliverance, yet I never knew them?"

I woke up from the dream alarmed and startled. I said to the Holy Spirit, "So there are not only people who will perform signs, wonders, and miracles who will be sent to hell, but also people who receive all these things who will also be in hell. Why?" Immediately the Holy Spirit spoke again to me and said, "Because those who worked miracles, prophesied, and cast out demons never preached the full gospel of Jesus Christ, which is the message of repentance. They were so in love with the gifts that I had given them that people became trophies and souvenirs to them. When My power would manifest in their ministries, they would tell people that I loved them, but never that they needed to repent for their sins. I tell you that a great deception will sweep over the signs and wonders movement in the earth. Beware of the ministries where miracles and prophecies will flow, but the message of repentance is a no go. You have been warned." Then I woke up.

Will you pray with me today that ministers and individuals who move in God's power will not only live a lifestyle of repentance but also preach it? What if people getting healed, delivered, and prophesied to and only told God loves them isn't the full gospel message? What if repentance and holiness is the full gospel message too?

## LET THE CLEANSING AND IGNITING COME

An urgent wakeup call is being released in the contemporary prophetic movement. It's time to arouse from our slumber. Our greatest days are truly ahead of us! A mighty cleansing and igniting is coming. The prophets and prophetic people must be pure and full of the fire of God. Great hope and vision will mark the days we live in, but so will a spirit of sobriety and deep repentance.

The call to the secret place will far surpass any desire for a platform or microphone. A generation of Jeremiah 23 prophets and prophetic people are emerging for such a time as this. Encounters on the road to Emmaus are waiting. The prophets and prophetic people have heard the clarion call to stand in the counsel of the Lord and hear His word. Now is the time to respond and make ourselves ready.

Will you answer the call?

# AFTERWORD

**S**OMETHING is about to shift in the prophetic world. A cleansing is imminent. As this purification of much that has been impure takes root, it will also include a changing of the guard. While faithful patriarchs such as John Paul Jackson, Bishop Bill Hamon and my own father John Sandford (to name a few) have paved the way for reliable prophetic ministry, it seems clear that a fresh set of voices will now carry it forward. An older generation is passing away or simply fading from the spotlight while a fresh group of anointed prophets are just beginning to emerge.

While I am not saying there was anything less than godly in those now fading from the spotlight or in those now gone home to glory, and while I am certainly not minimizing the contributions they made to the body of Christ, I am saying that the generation now emerging carries a fresh heart. These will speak more from humble intimacy with Jesus and from a pastoral spirit than from a concern for gifting. Their words will flow more from the heart of the Father than from any felt need to prophesy, build a great ministry, or stand on anyone's stage. More than developing their gifts, they will seek oneness with Jesus and His nature. They will pursue rest in relationship with Him more than being supernatural.

The aforementioned pioneers pointed the way with an emphasis on character, the Cross, and biblical grounding, but their foundational core messages were, in my opinion, too little heard by too many who needed to listen. In this coming generation, however, the call to integrity, character, and solid biblical grounding has been heeded. The need to wow the body of Christ and tickle the ears of men is giving way to a hunger to bow before the King of Kings, broken by His love and faithful to His words, regardless of the fallout. As a result, these emerging prophets will release into the people of God a deeper level of life than we have known, as well as a sense of liberty in holiness that is both life-giving and free of condemnation.

We older ones whom God allows to remain—some of us perhaps late maturers in matters prophetic, hidden by the hand of God until now—inherit a calling to father the coming movement. The heart of a true father desires to see sons and daughters grow into greater things than he could ever attain. Those into whom we sow life and wisdom may therefore carry greater gifting and walk in a higher level of revelation than we who are called to be fathers have known, but so did Elisha exercise a greater level of raw anointing than did his spiritual father, Elijah.

What if those in this emerging generation become better known than those of us called to father them? What if their books sell more than ours? What if they stand before thousands as we merely watch and pray? Can we walk in the kind of humility that rejoices to see others gaining notice and recognition for their full-grown wisdom and the revelations for which we sowed the seeds in hidden places? Will our hearts swell with pleasure and pride in their advancement? Or will old wineskins and unredeemed elements of character, ambition, and insecurity disqualify us and hinder us from delivering and releasing the fullness of the treasure God has entrusted to us for their sake?

When these younger voices confront abuses and imbalances in prophetic ministries, will an older, more established prophetic community receive and judge their words on the basis of the humble spirit in which they are delivered and the soundness of their biblical grounding? Or will there be rejection and backlash with cries of, "Who does that young guy think he is, correcting and rebuking major internationally known ministries?!" The apostle Paul exhorted young Timothy not to allow anyone to look down on him for his youth, but rather to exercise the gifting, anointing, and authority imparted to him through the laying on of Paul's hands. Will an older generation need to be exhorted regarding the flip side of Paul's admonition so that, in fact, the older generation does *not* despise the younger for being what I might call "chronologically handicapped"?

The shift underway in the prophetic world has only just begun. It will unfold in two waves over time: 1) The passing and/or retirement of an older generation and the emergence of a fresh and mostly younger one, and 2) a cleansing of prophetic ministry to discredit and eliminate pollutions and abuses across a broad front. We need, and we will have, a more accurate flow of prophetic ministry in the body of Christ, faithful to the Father's heart in Jesus. God our Father will see to it for the vindication of His own name.

Young voices like Jeremiah Johnson's have been raised up by our Lord to sound the alarm and raise the cry. Listen to his heart and words. You won't be sorry you did!

R. Loren Sandford
Senior Pastor of Newsong Church and Ministries
Author of *Purifying the Prophetic* and
*Understanding Prophetic People*

# NOTES

## CHAPTER 6 THE PROPHET'S PROFILE

1. See https://aword.info/tag/a-w-tozer, accessed July 24, 2018.

## CHAPTER 14 A VISION OF THE COMING DAYS

1. R. Loren Sandford, *The Prophetic Church: Wielding the Power to Change the World* (Grand Rapids, MI: Chosen Books, 2009), 16.

2. Frank Bartleman, *Azusa Street: An Eyewitness Account to the Birth of the Pentecostal Revival* (New Kensington, PA: Whitaker House, 2000), 19.

# ABOUT JEREMIAH JOHNSON

JEREMIAH JOHNSON planted and serves on the eldership team at Heart of the Father Ministry in Lakeland, Florida. A gifted teacher, prophet, and multiple book author, Jeremiah travels extensively throughout the United States and abroad as a conference and guest speaker. Jeremiah is also the founder and director of Maranatha School of Ministry. MSM is a full-time five-fold ministry training center that equips and sends out end-time messengers. For more information visit jeremiahjohnson.tv. Jeremiah and his wife, Morgan, have four children.